MARFA

MAR

THE TRANSFORMATION
OF A WEST TEXAS TOWN

CHARLES N. PROTHRO TEXANA SERIES

RFA

KATHLEEN SHAFER

UNIVERSITY OF TEXAS PRESS ❤ AUSTIN

Copyright © 2017 by the University of Texas Press
All rights reserved
Printed in the United States of America
First edition, 2017
First paperback reprint, 2022

Requests for permission to reproduce material
from this work should be sent to:
Permissions
University of Texas Press
P.O. Box 7819
Austin, TX 78713-7819
utpress.utexas.edu/rp-form

The paper used in this book meets the minimum
requirements of ANSI/NISO Z39.48-1992
(R1997) (Permanence of Paper). ∞

Design by Lindsay Starr

Library of Congress Cataloging-in-Publication Data
Names: Shafer, Kathleen, 1979–, author.
Title: Marfa : the transformation of a West Texas town /
    Kathleen Shafer.
Other titles: Charles N. Prothro Texana series.
Description: First edition. | Austin : University of Texas Press,
    2017. | Series: Charles N. Prothro Texana series | Includes
    bibliographical references and index.
Identifiers: LCCN 2017018507| ISBN 978-1-4773-1831-7 (pbk.
    : alk. paper) | ISBN 978-1-4773-1439-5 (library e-book) |
    ISBN 978-1-4773-1440-1 (non-library e-book)
Subjects: LCSH: Marfa (Tex.)—History. | Landscape
    architecture—Texas—Marfa. | Arts—Texas—Marfa. |
    Arts—Economic aspects—Texas—Marfa. | Judd, Donald,
    1928–1994.
Classification: LCC F394.M296 S53 2017 | DDC
    976.4/933—dc23
LC record available at https://lccn.loc.gov/2017018507

doi:10.7560/314388

FOR MY SIBLINGS

CONTENTS

MARFA

CHAPTER 1

INTRODUCTION

□

It takes a long time to get to Marfa.

From El Paso, it's a relatively easy three-hour drive southeast down Highway 10 to Route 90. El Paso isn't a terribly large city, but once you've arrived at the airport, you're eager to get away from the noise and onto the great wide strip of highway that leads straight into the heart of West Texas.[1] There are roughly 120 miles to cover on 10, a bland American road that, like much of the greater American highway system, is distinguished only by its surrounding topography. Highways themselves are not immediately interesting, but they are literal gateways to areas that are; they are part of the journey. Getting to Marfa is a journey.

The colors in West Texas have a limited spectrum, but the blues, yellows, and greens are endless. The bright sun blanches the yellows in the grasses, making them resemble the color of old newspaper. Someone in Marfa told me that the shaft of the blue grama grass reflects light differently depending on the time of year, and this wonderfully reasonable explanation offers a lovely way to understand the somewhat inexplicable quality of light that characterizes this part of Texas.

The greens of the mesquite and desert shrub change with the seasons and are dependent on rainfall. Actually, a lot of things here are dependent on rainfall. Texas is driest at this western extremity, receiving less than 16 inches of rainfall per year,[2] and this aridity has crafted a quality of roughness in the flora and fauna, not to mention the folks. Survival here is a learned skill.

As you glance up at the big sky every so often, a relentlessly changing blue unfolds before you. At first bright, overexposed, it turns softer and deeper as the day turns to dusk. Perfectly sized cumulous and waves of cirrus clouds adorn the sky in seemingly never-ending rows.

Once you turn off of Highway 10 onto Route 90 and continue south, you don't pass too many cars on the two-lane road down to Marfa. The largest town you will pass on this 70-mile stretch of 90 is Valentine, but "town" is a generous term. Valentine was a water stop on the Southern Pacific Railroad, founded in 1881.[3] Today, its population lingers far below two hundred, and it fills only half a page in the *West of the Pecos* phone directory. It might be annotated on a map, but like every town in this part of West Texas, it doesn't have much going on that you can see. Whatever is happening usually happens behind closed doors, safe from Texas's intense climate.

It's easy to miss a lot of the detail, because details in the landscape of the West can blend together into a collective emptiness, and driving exacerbates this. When you actively look, however, there are things to notice: the rusted and abandoned farming equipment; the small structures that are so romantically decaying, their faded and cracked paint creating a visual record of passing time; the cloud of dust thrown up by a truck driving out in the ranchland. A modest Airstream nestled well off the highway becomes a gleaming landmark, and tumbleweeds skirt across the pavement. Even in a landscape this barren there is ample evidence of life and of activity, only it is spread out and often camouflaged by speed. A ranch home near the highway is more than just a house, for its imprint has extended well past any formal yard.

Here, there is no need to contain anything.

Cars parked in the lawn slowly become ornamental, and children's plastic and metal toys are carelessly left wherever. Their bright colors pop against the grass and dirt, and in an instant they are gone as you drive past. Some relics you miss by not peregrinating at leisure: old glass Coke bottles, beer cans rusted beyond legibility, a cattle carcass, one left shoe. While one cactus is decomposing, another is blooming and vibrant. Lizards dash around as you interrupt their otherwise undisturbed landscape.

You are sure to notice an odd building in Valentine because it seems so out of place in this land. On the west side of the road at the northern tip of Valentine is a small structure that belongs in New York's Soho neighborhood—not in remote West Texas. It is a Prada storefront, architecturally identical to its cosmopolitan sisters, and its sparse interior has authentic Prada footwear and handbags on display. There is no way to enter this small, pale structure, and there are no mannequins or employees. There is, however, a revolving cycle of graffiti from visitors and locals ("Dumb" is a nicely succinct one),[4] something that the structure's creators, Michael Elmgreen and Ingar Dragset, had anticipated, but the frequency of graffiti and the structure's decay are happening faster than they had imagined. To add insult to injury, bullet markings have even appeared on the thick polycarbonate windows (replacements for the original plate glass that was quickly vandalized)[5] that very clearly say "fuck you" to the highbrow art culture that has invaded Marfa. It's a gift from the locals who don't appreciate the irony behind a falsified Prada storefront "in the middle of nowhere."

Prada Marfa is a permanent installation by the aforementioned artists, completed in 2005 with the sponsorship of Ballroom Marfa and Art Production Fund, the former a nonprofit art space in Marfa and the latter a nonprofit art-commissioning fund based in New York. The minimalism of this storefront mirrors the minimalism that you will soon encounter in Marfa, and in this way the installation prepares you for the town you have traveled to see (at least, if you are coming from the west). It is an anomaly, a strange, specific object; it is something that does not belong, and yet, there it is. It is a tourist attraction in a distant, desolate landscape, as is Marfa.

Prada Marfa has become the background for countless photos, the backdrop of memories, a cultural marker to the traveling tourist. The installation signifies place, and thus any photo taken of it or using it as a background messages a sense of ownership or accomplishment: *I've been there*. Tourism is, after all, about consuming. Were one to take another photo, but without *Prada Marfa* in the background (perhaps facing the other side of the highway), the association to Marfa and to art is lost. Just like a photo in front of the White House or the Statue of Liberty signifies the places of Washington and New York, respectively, a photo in front of *Prada Marfa* signifies the place of Marfa.

What's most curious about *Prada Marfa* is that it is not in Marfa. Rather, it's about 36 miles from the town. Although the art display is closer to Valentine, the artists distinctly wanted their work to carry the name Marfa.[6] This is an important point, because Marfa is no longer just the name of a town. Marfa is a style, an identity, a character, and *Prada Marfa* is one of the first acts of commodification of Marfa under the auspices of high art. Marfa's identity is unsurprisingly a compilation of its history: a transition from cow town to art town to tourist town, and today it is all three of these at once, but these facets of the place can conflict with one another.

The sculpture has been troubled since its installation due to vandalism and the area's intense climate, and in 2013 it found itself at the center of a Texas Department of Transportation (DOT) controversy regarding roadside advertising. Then, in 2014 it was vandalized to somewhat resemble a Toms shoe store,[7] and early in 2016 Valentine's fellow West Texas town, Marathon, became the site of a Target Marathon store.[8] It's not so much art imitating life as it is art imitating art. Yes, West Texas has become meta.

The attraction of *Prada Marfa* has come to signify the cultural change that has taken place in Marfa. By its placement out there in the desert, the art puts a spotlight on Marfa and thus feeds its growing tourism industry. What results is a town composed of residents drawn to the isolation and charms of Marfa but who are witnessing a continued exportation of Marfa to the outside world, making them as a whole less isolated. In fact, it puts them and their town in a bubble to be gawked at and studied by outsiders like me.

Still, most locals aren't terribly concerned about *Prada Marfa*. After many conversations, it has become clear that most folks have

Prada Marfa, 2011.

Target Marathon, 2016.

essentially no opinion of *Prada Marfa*—they don't like it and they don't hate it (although some do like it, and some most definitely hate it). To me, it is refreshing that many Marfans don't care about it one way or the other, as if my asking them about it is a waste of their time. These folks who don't care, well, they just have other things to think about. This reminds me that although Marfa may be presented to the outside world as a "quirky artsy"[9] place—and certainly the outside world projects this identity onto Marfa—plenty of folks here have no association with that part of Marfa's identity. The place means different things to different people.

The slogan of the Marfa Visitor Center is this: Marfa: Tough to get to. Tougher to explain. But once you get here, you get it.

Well, let's hope so.

Marfa and Presidio County were put "on the art-world map"[10] by one person, the artist Donald Judd. Although Marfa's identity has changed in the years since his 1994 death, with incoming residents and foundations adding to the cultural landscape, Judd can unequivocally be credited with fronting Marfa's cultural change. No, he didn't do the kind of community investments that later residents would, but as an established and successful artist, he set the foundation. He built a museum in Marfa.

I spoke with the historian Cecilia Thompson in 2011 about Marfa. Thompson, who has since passed away, is the author of *History of Marfa and Presidio County, Texas, 1535–1946* from 1985 and, with Louis O'Connor, coauthor of *Marfa and Presidio County, Texas: A Social, Economic, and Cultural Study 1937–2008*, Volume 1 and Volume 2, both from 2014.

A sharp, wickedly smart old lady, and nearly blind when I met her, Cecilia knew the workings of Marfa and its environs like no other. She was raised on a ranch outside of Fort Davis, and after spending most of her life elsewhere, came back to the area to take care of her ailing parents. In 1982 she was commissioned to write the area's history, and she has observed and experienced the changes in Marfa since that time. I asked her what the town was like in the 1970s and '80s.

"Marfa was dead, dead, dead," she told me. "Judd had been here, but that didn't make much difference in the town activity. Even after his death the activity at the museum continued to build and to create relations with the community that Don had not done."

Judd, a legendary artist, left a legacy in both the museum that he created, the Chinati Foundation, and in his private living and work spaces in both Marfa and New York, now managed by the Judd Foundation. The members of these organizations work to maintain his creations for future generations. This has not always been an easy process, but at present the wheels seem to grease themselves. The success, as it were, of Marfa currently runs on its own popularity. The town has developed into a remarkable center of tourism.

It is in fact largely due to the earlier efforts of the Chinati and Judd Foundations, as well as to members of the Marfa community, that Marfa has become the sort of destination that it is. Marfa's present identity is more and more that of a tourist mecca, which can be looked at from economic and cultural perspectives and—depending on who you talk to—the positive and negative (or rather, complicated) implications of both. Change happens, and it has happened in Marfa. This change continues to fascinate me, and I have a great respect for this small town. I am an observer and a participant, and I am interested in exploring Marfa's sense of place.

"Judd introduced the area to the art world," Cecilia told me.

"Was that a good thing?"

"Yes. It saved it. The ranch culture had just faded away. We have inherited from them, so far as the town is concerned, these wonderful buildings and the wide streets and the courthouse—the physical structure basically came as a result of the ranchers' thinking and their production. And the larger homes in the northwest part of town are ranch homes. Many of them have sold, and there are a number of widows closeted in several of them."

I imagine these widows, sitting in their homes reading the local weekly newspaper, wondering what the hell has happened to their Marfa. I imagine what will happen when they've all passed away and that part of Marfa's history is no longer accessible.

"The ranch economy has been very poor. The ranchers are victims of drought. It is still basically a ranching community, in essence, although there isn't much presence of ranchers anymore." I'm intrigued by her comment. A ranching community without the presence of ranchers. So is it that the idea of this historic Marfa continues to permeate the town? As evidenced by the men I see in town in their Stetsons and Wranglers, driving pickup trucks, it is clear that ranching—despite a suffering economy—is still part of the cultural makeup of Marfa. But it has made way for the new cultural landscape, that of art. It's the combination of these two factors that defines this new Marfa identity.

Following his death in 1994, Judd quickly became something of a holy figure in the modern art community. Since that time, the journey to Marfa has become a pilgrimage of sorts for both artists and art patrons. It's a must-see for artists and nonartists alike. After Judd's death, the Chinati Foundation and the Judd Foundation were tasked with the responsibility of maintaining Judd's museum and his personal collections and properties, respectively—safeguarding his artistic vision—and this work largely revolves around what he did in Marfa. These organizations, constantly active in their duties, *produce* the space of Judd's Marfa. They work to maintain Marfa's material landscape as well as promote particular ways of seeing, imagining, and representing this space. And they also promote certain ways of inhabiting Marfa, which bring together both the material (or the real) and the ideal Marfa.[11] What I mean by this is that while Marfa has a presence in a world much larger than its own borders, it is also in many ways just a small town in West Texas. In fact, those who come to Marfa, either as tourists or transplants, don't always seem to realize just how small this town really is. In this way the real Marfa and the ideal Marfa are two separate things. The real Marfa is, perhaps, an unknown land to many outsiders, and the ideal Marfa is what outsiders often project onto Marfa.

Marfa is not a given space, because all space is created. Marfa's existence and identity are directly owed to the people of its history, including but certainly not limited to Donald Judd. Marfa is an active, engaging space that continues to transform, most notably through its tourism but also through the arrival of newcomers. What's more, the artistic side of Marfa has come to mean more than Donald Judd. Marfa is saturated with talent, be it in visual art, film, music, writing, or more—the list is long. Once in line to become a ghost town, present-day Marfa is anything but. It has even appeared in a list of the best small towns in America, as well as being deemed a "place to go," according to the *New York Times* in 2016.[12] That said, Marfa's geographic remoteness almost guarantees that its population will never exceed about two thousand residents. The distance between Marfa and elsewhere is the filter that keeps it somewhat protected from any dramatic development, but nevertheless it continues to be a changing town.

"There's no industry," Cecilia told me. "Since the housing rush here, and the high raise of prices, few local workers can find housing here now." Many people who work in Marfa drive in from surrounding Alpine, Fort Davis, or Presidio.

As a result of the careful maintenance and nurturing of culture, countless newspaper and magazine articles are published on Marfa each year, and a growing body of documentary pieces, both film and oral, is being produced.[13] People are simply curious about this town. Writers from publications such as the *New York Times*, *Texas Monthly*, and *Travel and Leisure*[14] compose features that mull over Marfa's art and the strangeness of the town, but none reach a satisfying conclusion. In the words of one resident, "Most of the articles get it wrong." Some of the articles insist on a divided Marfa: rich and poor, art and nonart, Hispanic and white. As with any culture, the workings of Marfa are much more complicated than simple binary divisions.

I asked Cecilia what she thought about these different types of residents—the ranchers, the newcomers and artists, and the Hispanics.

"The Hispanic community is as old if not older than the ranching community because the ranchers could not have succeeded without the help of the Hispanic community."

I ask her about the Hispanic community engaging with the art one.

"The Hispanic community unfortunately does not join into the art activities, although they would be welcome."

She tells me that the native ranching community keeps separate and apart. My thoughts go back to the widows in the large old ranch homes.

Marfa is a dangerous place for someone like me. I'm an introvert and a loner, and I generally have no problem spending days alone without direct contact with people. That might be where the appeal lies to outsiders who travel here for bits of time. If you're a writer, you can write. If you're an artist, you can make art. If you're a lost soul, you may come here thinking you will find yourself. At best, you may do your thing and no one will bother you. At worst, you may suffocate from the stillness. Here, there is a lot of space and a lot of nothing, so the little things become big things. It's what makes Marfa so enchanting but also what protects it from too much growth. New folks show up in town frequently, but they don't stay permanently.

I've been here on and off for six years, exploring and writing and talking and researching and generally pondering the place that is Marfa, Texas. At times, I've retreated into myself and my quiet adobe house (sublets, always) and asked myself how these people get by out here, without so many of the small luxuries that I've long been accustomed to, living in Austin. But I suppose a book about the things that Marfa lacks wouldn't be terribly interesting, so instead I've been looking at everything that Marfa does have, and I embrace the many lovely qualities to be found here.

I've come to really like these people of Marfa, these Marfans. That sounds like an alien name, and in a way, it is fitting. Marfans are unwaveringly friendly, as are the folks of the neighboring yet remarkably different towns of Fort Davis, Alpine, Marathon, Terlingua, and Presidio. Everyone here has a story, and a history, but they aren't braggers. In fact, I've found most residents to be modest about their lives and their accomplishments. They are proud of Marfa but also protective of it, if not concerned for how tourism has changed this place and will continue to do so.

Marfa is geographically remote, and there isn't a lot of work to be found. Housing is an issue because of the tourism and second-home ownership that leads to short-term Airbnb rentals and contributes to a lack of affordable housing for locals. Marfa's cultural landscape includes a historic yet possibly dying ranching community, cyclically plagued by drought. After two military installations (Fort D. A. Russell and Marfa Army Airfield) closed at the end of World War II, followed by the seven-year drought of the 1950s, Marfa's population dwindled as locals moved away.

Today, Marfa is a vibrant town that attracts tourists in all seasons and a regular (it seems to me) rotation of new residents. Marfa is a far cry from the ghost town that it could have become.

Marfa is an international destination, and that fact provides locals and tourists with a form of cultural capital. Pierre Bourdieu[15] was the first to use this term to make a distinction between economic, social, and cultural forms of capital. To be a part of Marfa on various artistic terms is to gain this cultural capital. To have performed live music at the funeral-home-turned-live-music-venue-and-bar Padre's (now closed), or to have been given a writing residency at the Lannan Foundation (invitation only), or an artist residency at the Chinati Foundation (it receives between 150 and 350 applicants each year for a handful of slots), and so on can be a valued component of one's CV. And, because of Marfa's small size, it is common for artists to be interviewed on Marfa Public Radio (an NPR affiliate that began broadcasting in 2006) or profiled in the *Big Bend Sentinel* as a visiting artist, writer, or scholar. Economic changes in Marfa can be assessed in terms of tourism and taxes, but apart from those, the cultural capital that pervades this small ranching community is something that cannot be denied.

Many residents tout Marfa's unique placement as a cultural center as a reason to live here. Between the programming of the Chinati and Judd Foundations, Ballroom Marfa, the Crowley Theater, the independent bookstore (Marfa Book Company), and the Lannan Foundation, among others, one can see authors, musicians, and other artists throughout any given week. While this would not be anything special in a larger city, it is remarkable in a town boasting a population that hovers around two thousand residents.

Marfa is sometimes referred to as an artist's mecca or an artist's colony, and while it is a mecca of sorts for the arts religious, an artist's colony implies an intention that I believe is lacking in Marfa. Its growth has been organic and largely unplanned, and many of its residents don't want it to become "another Santa Fe." (Marfa is far too small to be compared to Santa Fe, but Taos is an apt comparison.) Further, Marfa is, in many regards, just another small town, but its transformation over the past thirty years has undoubtedly altered its identity from both a local and tourist vantage point. The destination, for many, is the experience of permanent art installations, but there is more to Marfa than art. I do love the art here, but I also want to know more about the town removed from the art. I want to know what its residents are up to and what they think about the changes they are witnessing.

For example, the awe-inspiring Marfa Mystery Lights—unexplained phenomena that draw tourists and conspiracy theorists alike—have been attracting visitors since long before Judd. Marfa is also a destination for glider pilots and hunters, as well as one of many stops on a drive to Big Bend National Park or the McDonald Observatory in Fort Davis. Still, the placing of Marfa to the outside world has focused attention on this one aspect of its identity (the art), and because of its success, other towns are seeking to mimic what Marfa has become. In the past few years, it has been suggested that towns like Archer City, Texas; Green Mountain Falls, Colorado; and Winslow, Arizona, can become destinations like Marfa.[16]

Unfortunately, there is no formula for this. Many factors, including hard work, came together to create what we now know as Marfa. This Marfa teeters on a line of polished minimalism on one side and casual laissez-faire vernacular on the other—a new and an old Marfa, if you will. To sway too much to one side would alter the place of Marfa, which is a balance of both these styles and attitudes, and the town must work to figure out what this means for its people, to maintain the fabric of its community.

I read, listen to, and watch every media piece on Marfa. I consume them heartily because I am always interested in what is being written about Marfa, about the recent goings-on as they relate to the ongoing tourism. I've noticed that the language used to portray

Marfa in many newspaper and magazine stories has implied aggression (clash, mafia, mob, stampedes, showdown, flocking) or increasingly moves toward an implication of culture and place (cool, scene, oasis, mecca, modernist, laid-back). Each story's focus continues to build on the outsider's perspective of Marfa[17] and thereby creates another avenue for cultural dissemination.

I believe that Marfa's placement on the cultural map is tied to its vast landscape and quality of light, because it is these two factors that people often speak of when discussing their affection for Marfa. It's what has influenced and what continues to influence so many residents and visitors. For the residents of Marfa who have little interest in participating in the various artistic and cultural events (and there are many of them), their Marfa is a very different place. When I first began my research on Marfa, I thought it was appropriate, if not convenient, to divide the residents into three main groups: Hispanics, ranchers, and artists. I knew this was an oversimplification but thought it was the easiest way to try to explain the place of Marfa to someone not familiar with it. The more I got to know Marfa, however, the more I knew that this division was inaccurate, and I don't want to force the complexity of the residents' identities into three neat categories. Not everyone in Marfa is a rancher or an artist or Hispanic, or only one and not any other. Marfa is no different from any town where different kinds of people are doing different kinds of things.

What I hope you will gain from reading this book is a modern rendering of geography's "terra incognita,"[18] or the unknown land. "Whether or not a particular area may be called 'unknown' depends both on knowledge and on what kind of knowledge is taken into account."[19] To Marfans, their home is a known land. To outsiders, it is a mysterious land. You can reasonably deduce information from what you know about West Texas: the climate, the altitude, the proximity to Mexico. But to make an unknown land known involves imagination. "An imaginative conception is essentially a new vision, a new creation, and consequently the less imaginative we are the less fresh and original will be our writing . . . and the less effective in stimulating the imaginations of others."[20] My research on Marfa has taken an imaginative approach, specifically because I have been interested in making a connection between the geographer's concept of landscape, space, and place and Judd's writing of space, and I explore these three terms in depth later. But I've also come to Marfa with an open mind and a relentless curiosity about the makings of its culture. I don't want to write another magazine piece on Marfa. I want to delve into the space itself, to describe it, explain it, and contemplate its various components. I want to be honest, and curious, and respectful, but I'm not interested in doting on Marfa. The town has struggles just like any other.

There may be no place yet uncovered in literal terms, but there are always new ways to approach an understanding of the landscape that surrounds us. Marfa in particular is an ideal place of study because its small physical size stands in marked contrast to its significant cultural footprint. Further, despite its popularity and growing international presence, Marfa is in many ways still an unknown land to outsiders—still in many ways a frontier town. It is a place that wants to hold on to its history as a ranching community in a landscape that has been devastated by this same industry. It is a place whose beauty inspired a world-renowned artist to move here and explore alternative and permanent ways of exhibiting art and to do so while considering the surrounding landscape and available architecture. It is a place populated mostly by Hispanics, whose experience of Marfa is not the focus of the media's attention. It is a place near the border with Mexico, which has contributed to its history and present occupation by the US Customs and Border Protection. It is a place of change, and although all places are places of change, Marfa is special.

Why is it special? It is hard for me to articulate at times. Maybe it's because I don't want to put it on a pedestal, as I feel others have, because in so many ways it is just another town. Maybe it's only special because outsiders say it's special. Maybe its residents don't like people calling their town special.

I told someone here recently that I was writing a book on Marfa.

"You should write about Alpine—it's much more interesting."

Alpine is interesting, and very different from Marfa, while being just two dozen miles away and in another county. But Alpine doesn't have the brand recognition that Marfa does. And that goes all the way back to Donald Judd.

Marfa's popularity and outsider interest will continue to attract additional academic investigations by future scholars,[21] and in particular I hope that a native or local will write his or her own story of Marfa that will add new perspectives and experiences, or perhaps completely disagree with everything that I have written. Any mistakes herein are my own, and I am always interested in gathering new information to help inform my positions.

Marfa is a shifting place, and its smallness and uniqueness have come together to create a special appeal to tourists. People come to Marfa for the land and for the light, which are vast, intense, and mesmerizing. In Cecilia's words, "I think that what people have come to Marfa for they will always come for and that is the sky, the clear atmosphere, the space, and that it has a reputation for being very friendly. And those things will still exist. And they will still attract people. What are they looking for? Peace, quiet, a place to work. And a friendly atmosphere."

CHAPTER 2

THE HISTORY OF MARFA

☐

There is something very special about getting up and going outside to walk in a landscape in any place one visits, but it's especially true in Marfa. In West Texas, each step against the rugged terrain is a fight against a dry and hard ground, for the desert shrub is dense and stubborn. The sun is a constant source of brightness, and there is no shade anywhere. Without a hat, a long-sleeved shirt, and water, a day spent outside can be dangerous, even deadly.

The first time I traveled to Marfa, I was photographing abandoned airfields in the West, including the long-abandoned Marfa Army Airfield, which is just east of town and south of the Marfa Lights Viewing Center. I am drawn to the crumbling runways and cement foundations that are all but hidden to someone who doesn't know they are there. Before my first visit, I was able to track down the ranch manager to ask his permission—most land in the region (and all of Texas, really) is private, and much of it is owned by absentee landlords who lease it out for grazing. At the end of our brief phone call, he warned, "Don't call me if you get bit by a rattler." During my repeated visits, I've been able to track different areas of the airfield, always seeing something new or something in a new way than before. As I walked around the space, alone and under the bright sun, I got to know the landscape.

One early morning on my third trip to the airfield, I am climbing up and over the fence in a corner of the viewing center area, careful not to tear my jeans on the barbed wire. It's just past 7:30 a.m. and about 70 degrees. I secure my sun hat and start my trot south. The only distraction is a fly that tails me for nearly the entire two hours I am out in the field. The farther I walk into the landscape, the fainter becomes the sound of cars passing on the highway, and eventually I am left with only the sounds of my walking, the flapping of crows' wings overhead, and the scuttle of small and hurried lizards at my feet. Each sound is an echo, and my ears slowly adjust.

They can't be seen from the highway, but an endless number of building foundation pieces—perfectly small concrete soldiers, evenly spaced—and some crumbling walls line up in rows throughout the field. The army may have been quick to remove buildings, but it didn't do the best clean-up job. During my walk, I pass a plethora of cattle and antelope waste; it's a good measure to determine how long the land has been out of the grazing cycle and which animal breeds currently occupy it. I've got to look down half the time to avoid stepping in the droppings.

As I come to the ramp where the planes were parked, and where a fence now divides grazing areas, I see six horses, one with a young colt, drinking from a trough and sweeping their tails. When they see me, their eyes lock on me, alert—perhaps because of the colt, or perhaps because it's not often that a stranger walks by them, out in their land. They cannot stop staring at me, patiently watching. They appear to be afraid of me, so I hook widely around their space to imply that I am not a threat. Then, in two quick moves, I am over the barbed-wire fence and my feet touch the concrete of the former plane ramp.

I walk straight down the ramp, due south, and toward the first runway. The trees here are taller, fuller, reaching 6 feet or more above me. Then I walk northwest on the runway and turn north to meet back up with the ramp. I'm at the northern end of what was the west side of the installation by the remnants of the hangars. It always amazes me to see the iron, glass, and brick left there without

Foundation pieces at the Marfa Army Airfield, 2011.

concern, but these castaways are something I appreciate. I take a few iron wheel joints from the hangar door mechanism to add to my collection—at this point it is a ritual—and observe the many red bricks scattered on the ground, "GROESBECK REDS" stamped on their faces. This and a broken network of asphalt runways is all that's left of what was once a large military installation.

I head over to one of my favorite places on the airfield: a large slab of concrete at the very southeastern edge of the installation, near a set of train tracks. On this slab rest the remains of a building, also concrete. I've not been able to determine what purpose the building had, but I imagine it could have been a meeting site for the train. At some point in recent years it became a temporary shelter, for clothing remnants and other markers of habitation are scattered around. Curiously, one large wall and one smaller corner wall section remain, too stubborn and strong to come down. (Why only these fragments? Was the rest torn down? Did it fall down? How does the large wall stand on its own?) The walls are big enough that I imagine a comfortable single-family home could have been here. If I stand all the way back at the highway, and know what I am looking for, I can see these remains. Whenever I drive from Alpine toward Marfa, I always look for the large wall, as if it is a lighthouse bringing me to safety.

The fullness of the wall rises and falls as I move around it, changing my perspective, and the sun's light creates shadows that further change the appearance of the shapes. When I stand to the east of the structure, exactly parallel to the large wall, it no longer looks like a one-sided building. The completeness of the wall plays a visual trick, and the structure appears intact. As I walk around the space, however, its completeness falls apart as the wall starts to thin, until finally, as I'm standing on the south side and exactly perpendicular to the wall, it looks like one tall, narrow piece of concrete, with the smaller piece standing out. The fullness of the large wall has vanished.

When I move over to the west side and again parallel to the wall, it looks more complete, although I can easily see that only these pieces are left of the structure, with the large base slab of concrete

The wall at Marfa Army Airfield, 2011.

in front of me. Lastly, to move north and look at the wall, now to my left and perpendicular to me, reduces it to another sliver of tall concrete.

I love this wall. It represents the need for me to constantly shift my perspective in order to see how different angles affect the way I understand a place. I think of how understanding Marfa also requires one to walk around all of its proverbial walls, to see all of its angles.

Before long I start to really feel the sun, so I head north toward the car. The Marfa Lights Viewing Center serves as the most prominent marker on my walk; without it anchoring me, I might have become lost out here. I pass a long-forgotten but still recognizable cobalt blue tetrahedron, used as a wind direction indicator, and think about its quality as a sculpture, think about how many years it has been out here undisturbed. The sun inches its way up the sky, and by the time I am back at the car it's already 88 degrees at 9:15 a.m. I can't imagine spending more than a couple of hours outside under the blazing sun. The light is so bright and so uniform in this wide space that it sometimes hurts my eyes. I head back to town to make breakfast.

While the history of Marfa the town begins with the railroad and with ranching, the geologic, Spanish, Mexican, and Native American histories had established the landscape of West Texas centuries before. "All history depends on earlier histories."[1]

Early Spanish colonists of the sixteenth century were the first European explorers in the area,[2] and they called the land "el despoblado," or "the uninhabited place." Before them, Comanche and Apache Native Americans had at various times occupied the area that is now Presidio County, but these tribes were largely nomadic and didn't establish themselves in the harsh landscape. Mexicans occupied parts of the area as well, despite the fact that the terrain was hostile to people and could support only small populations.[3]

That a landscape can be hostile to a person or people is an intriguing thought, as though the landscape itself is a wild animal, baring its teeth and growling to say, "Don't come near me." The landscape of West Texas, in my opinion, is beautiful but uninviting.

Or perhaps it's beautiful and deceitfully inviting, like a Venus flytrap. In some ways, the vastness of both the land and the sky defines a barrier to entry, as though the environment is simply too overwhelming to grasp or control.

Marfa is situated at the northern slant of the Chihuahuan Desert, an ecoregion that in the United States spans western Texas and parts of New Mexico and Arizona, and in Mexico spans the states of Chihuahua, Coahuila, Durango, Zacatecas, and Nuevo León. This desert region has little rainfall, harsh sun, and rugged terrain. The author Susan Tweit describes this wild animal best:

> Green is as rare as shade. The desert is neither soft nor appealing. Its shapes are hard and angular; the plants are studded with spines and thorns; the animals are armed with venom and stingers. Its disquieting landscape of huge spaces and its uncompromisingly harsh climate shrink humans and their work to a very, very small size.[4]

Marfa is more or less at the center of the Marfa Basin, the smallest piece of the larger Permian Basin, which characterizes most of West Texas. The land was part of an epeiric sea during the Cambrian to Mississippian periods. Today, some of the animals found in the area are the desert mule deer, the pronghorn, and, in mountainous areas, the Carmen Mountain whitetail, and the exotic aoudad. Elk, buffalo, badgers, porcupines, gray foxes, blue quails and Eurasian collared doves, javelina, coyotes, jackrabbits, desert tarantulas, and mountain lions occupy the area, along with many lizard and other bird species.

The Spanish colonists left the land largely ignored for years but, driven by expansion efforts, finally decided to establish a military presence in the seventeenth century. Their influence "effectively doomed"[5] the native tribes, and the military activity throughout the region dictates a large part of its history. ("Presidio" translated from Spanish means "fort," although it also has a curious secondary meaning of "prison." This would make Presidio County a place that either protects itself against the outside world, or perhaps imprisons its people [maybe that's another way to think about the vastness, not as something freeing but as something stifling].) West Texas remains one of the least populated areas of the United States,[6] and Presidio County is also one of the poorest.

In 1821, Mexico gained independence from Spain, and in 1836, Texas gained independence from Mexico. Texas joined the United States in 1845, and the Mexican-American War of 1846–1848 greatly altered the political development of the area. Before 1848, the state of Chihuahua occupied land much farther north than its current boundary, the Rio Grande. The Treaty of Guadalupe Hidalgo addressed the pressing matter of land ownership, but its language was brief and vague. Further, the United States rejected parts of the treaty, including an article that offered protection to Mexican citizens.[7] In 1848, the United States agreed to pay $15 million for its new land, and the Mexican Boundary Survey officially established the Rio Grande as the border between the two countries.[8] However, one could easily argue that this land, which had been occupied by native inhabitants for many generations, was stolen.

In 1883, the rancher Ralph Ellison was driving cattle toward Marfa from Alpine. At the base of the Chinati Mountains, at what is now known as Paisano Pass, he spotted strange lights flickering about in the darkness. While he believed these lights to be fires from the Apaches, neither he nor his crew was able to locate any tracks or remnants of fire the following day. Ellison didn't document this sighting in his journal, but oral tradition passed down his experience to generations of family members.[9] What became known as the "Marfa Mystery Lights" have been mystifying (and confounding) folks ever since.

An early written story of the lights appeared in 1945 in the *San Angelo Times*,[10] and there are other accounts from the pilots of the Marfa Army Airfield, who spotted them from the air but were unable to locate a source.[11] Says one pilot of a light, "We both had the distinct impression that it knew exactly where we were and that it was just daring us to chase it. It seemed to possess intelligence."[12]

Many books explore the proposed theories of the mystery lights and document a growing body of eyewitness accounts.[13] Newspaper articles have added to the lore throughout the years, never solving but always perpetuating the delightful mystery. Teams of scientists have traveled to the field with equipment, some advanced and some low-tech. The television show *Unsolved Mysteries*[14] has featured the unexplained lights, and a search on YouTube produces myriad low-resolution videos, mostly juvenile, that attempt to document and explain.

One local, Armando, told me how he had convinced the Chamber of Commerce in the 1980s that the mystery lights were something special, and that they should be advertised as something fun and different that tourists would travel to see. He went so far as to volunteer his time to drive visitors out from the hotel to see them. In 1986, Marfa held the first annual Marfa Lights Festival, which has taken place every Labor Day weekend since. That same year, the first roadside viewing area was built, which acted to centralize the onlookers and keep cars off of private ranch roads. The current viewing area was built in 2003, and on any given night people come for a chance to see the famous Marfa Mystery Lights.

The oldest legend to explain the lights is the legend of Alaste, who was the last Apache chief in the Big Bend. Alaste was tricked by the Mexicans and separated from his tribe, who were then slaughtered. The ghosts of this tribe are said to be signaling Alaste with their fires.[15] I've always liked this theory, not only because it predates the automobile—a common explanation of the lights—but also because it speaks to the activity and history of the area that predates Marfa itself.

Other theories relate to the area's more recent history: atomic military testing on the army airfield, which never happened; underground phosphorescent gas because of the geologic history of the Marfa plateau, but a source has never been found; some even propose that it is the residents of Marfa taking turns adventuring around the hills with flashlights (or attaching flashlights to jackrabbits) to attract tourism. This might be my favorite theory.

In 1975, a Sul Ross University physics class went in search of the lights but came to no conclusion.[16] In 1999, one of the students from this class, now a teacher himself, led another expedition of high school physics students, armed with low-tech tools to aid their research. This time, they determined that the lights' timing and

The viewing platform of the Marfa Lights Viewing Center, 2011.

frequency did correlate with automobiles weaving in and out of the mountain road where the lights are seen. In 2004, the University of Texas at Dallas chapter of the Society of Physics Students also went on the hunt for the lights, and concluded that the so-called mystery lights are indeed car headlights.

The obvious problem with the car headlights theory—apart from the fact that it takes all the fun out of it—is that cars weren't around in the nineteenth century, and during the war years gas was rationed, making frequent automobile use uncommon. Also, there are plenty of stories of seeing the lights up close and personal, and reports of the lights seeming to have a sort of intelligence about them—all of which must either humor or frustrate the scientists. Eyewitness accounts of seeing the lights up close, which are rare, have all noted that the lights seemed friendly, almost playful, and these witnesses report they almost never felt frightened or threatened.

The most likely explanation is that the Marfa Mystery Lights are a meteorological phenomenon.[17] This proposal holds that the lights are an illusion, caused by the layering of cool air on the ground and warm air above.[18] These opposing air densities bend light "like a lens"[19] to create these blinking lights that move about on the horizon. It's not unlike other weather phenomena such as St. Elmo's fire. The mirage of these projected lights could be sourced to the car headlights of the highway from Presidio to Marfa, or to other light sources. For all the fieldwork and attempts at explanation that various researchers have undertaken, most locals are content with the mystery of the lights. The mystery is a component of Marfa's identity that makes the place special (and exportable—Marfa's El Cosmico sells "See Mystery Lights" T-shirts).

It took me many attempts to see the lights, but I eventually saw them.

When I told Armando in 2011 that I had not yet seen the lights, he was flabbergasted. "You will see them with me," he said, determined. We got in my car and drove west of town to a ranch road. We slowly turned off the highway and headed south, the tires kicking up dirt in our wake. After a few minutes, Armando instructed me to stop the car. We both got out and turned to look back toward the Chinati Mountains. I remember feeling both nervous and excited, because being with a local would surely guarantee the lights' existence. After a few minutes of looking out into the distance, one light appeared, then another to the side of it. Armando was pleased. The lights flickered randomly back and forth, with no sense of timing or choreography. A third light appeared, closer to the second. The lights were dancing a simple and silly dance, and we were witnesses to it, just two people on the side of this dusty ranch road. Seeing the lights is to confirm their mystery and to embrace it.

The mystery lights vary in both size and color, but are most often said to be the size of baseballs, grapefruits, or basketballs when seen up close. They fluctuate in their luminosity, appearing to shift between dim and bright. The lights split and rejoin, as if playful, and they appear to shift color, from white to yellow to orange, and even red and blue and green. The lights can disappear and reappear in the same spot or elsewhere. Multiple lights often look like they are interacting with each other.

What is of most interest to me, as far as mysterious lights go, is that in a group of curious onlookers, some people will see the lights, and others won't. I think about the way we see things, how we see the landscape. But it's also about who is doing the seeing.[20] Seeing a landscape is not a given; it is an active process. If I can accept that sight is an imperfect, subjective tool, I can accept that there will be some things nearly impossible to explain and reconcile. The Marfa Mystery Lights are real, and strange, and unique to Marfa. I don't need answers or facts; it is their charm and mystery that I embrace.

Marfa was established in 1883 as a water stop on the expanding Southern Pacific Railroad that allowed goods and people to be imported, and cattle, wool, silver, and other goods to be exported. In the summer of 1881, the Galveston, Harrisburg, and San Antonio line was slowly creeping westward from San Antonio and eastward from El Paso in what became the third transcontinental railroad in the United States. This expansion provided needed access from farm to market for cattlemen and miners. White ranchers already settled in the Fort Davis area added more land to their holdings, first expanding cattle and later sheep herds. The original beef stock was primarily the Texas Longhorn but later included the Shorthorn (predictably, the Marfa High School mascot) and the prized Hereford.[21]

The railway line reached Marfa on January 16, 1882,[22] and was completed end to end in 1883. Marfa and other small towns of the Big Bend were literal water stops (also called tank towns) along the line because the steam engine needed a replenishment of water on a regular basis. Today, the geographic effects of this history can be measured by the remarkably consistent thirty-minute drive from one tank town to the next.

In March 1883, Marfa established a post office, with a town population of 150. Over the next two years, Marfa continued to grow, and in 1885 the county seat moved from Fort Davis to Marfa. A state contract was awarded to build the courthouse and the county jail. The courthouse is three and a half stories high, a Second Empire structure with four corner towers, mansard roofs, and a large Brunelleschi-like dome on octagonal drum/brick construction.[23] It's an incredibly beautiful building. The brick was made in Marfa, and the pinkish stone is native to Texas. Even today this whimsical structure is a visual anchor to the town, and the bird's-eye view from its dome gives a nice overview of the landscape.

By the turn of the century, Marfa had expanded into a prosperous shipping center of both sheep and cattle, and reached a population of 930 by 1900.[24] There were two hotels, two saloons, two churches, one fruit store, one lumberyard, one livery stable, one barber shop, two meat markets, one boot shop, one blacksmith, one woodworker, and one weekly newspaper.[25] Marfa was a trade and shipping center for other towns in the area, such as Terlingua, Shafter, and Ruidosa, and together they provided the rest of the country with beef and silver. In this way, Marfa was never localized. It was always a connecting point between West Texas and other parts of the state and country, and even to the rest of the world. Many tried for oil (and some still do), but in that regard Presidio County is a dry landscape.[26] In 1907, automobiles and electricity arrived, and one newspaper article described "Marfa, City of Lights"[27] with awe.

The Presidio County Courthouse, 2012.

In 1910, a group of Texas Rangers moved from Ysleta (now part of El Paso) to Marfa[28] due to an increasing conflict that became the Mexican Revolution.[29] The following year, the Third Cavalry arrived, and Camp Marfa was created as a semipermanent base for these troops. The men slept in tents until more permanent barracks could be built. From this time until the end of World War II, this military focus shaped Marfa's history, and today the Border Patrol continues to drive the military presence and contribute to Marfa's population and economy. (When driving toward Marfa north from Mexico or east from El Paso, you will be stopped at a Border Patrol station. You will be asked if you are an American citizen and where you are headed. The attendants have always been nice to me, if a little formal, but I know this is not always the case for other people.)

During the Mexican Revolution, which lasted until about 1920, many Mexicans seeking refuge traveled from Ojinaga, in Chihuahua, across the border to Presidio, Texas—today about an hour's drive from Marfa. The influx of Mexicans throughout Marfa's history, and particularly during this conflict, had a great impact on the area's identity and culture, and their assimilation into American life would not be without discrimination or conflict.[30] To walk along Marfa's main drag and see the names on buildings is to see the history of Marfa, but only its Anglo male history. Despite the hard work of the Mexican American men and women who helped turn the area into an economic and cultural presence, theirs is a history arguably lost or, at the very least, unattended to. To look beyond the main drag and skim through the small phone book or walk through the still-segregated cemeteries or even to look at simple census numbers is to see a dominant Hispanic presence in Marfa and its environs.[31] This presence largely began with the refugees from the Mexican Revolution, who landed in Marfa and mostly became agricultural laborers.

Both US Cavalry troops and Texas Rangers patrolled the area around Marfa for the next few years while various conflicts occurred along the border. Officially renamed Fort D. A. Russell in 1930, Camp Marfa was also known as Camp Albert and Camp US Troops, Marfa, Texas.[32] Both the Mexican Revolution and the United States' entrance into World War I in 1917 contributed to

Camp Marfa's growth, and in 1918 the government officially leased 420 acres from rancher W. G. Young for the more permanent establishment of the installation.[33] In 1927, the government purchased this land outright, and Camp Marfa's future as a permanent base was, for the time being, secured. In 1930, the name was changed to Fort D. A. Russell after David Allen Russell, a Civil War general killed in the Battle of Opequon in 1864.[34]

Air travel came to Marfa around this time as well—the present-day golf course is more or less where Royce Flying Field was—and the use of airplanes was an essential, efficient way of patrolling the border. Four hangars at this site were moved into town in the 1930s; Donald Judd purchased three of them, and the fourth eventually became the Holiday Inn Capri, now an events space and restaurant called The Capri. Marfa prospered during these years, not only because of the growing military economy but also because of the booming cattle industry, which benefited from the increased military presence. After all, the soldiers needed to eat and they needed wool and mohair for clothing.[35] Marfans knew that a military presence in town provided an economic advantage. They happily welcomed the soldiers, as evidenced by vintage newspaper articles, but didn't always appreciate the drinking, rowdiness, or "lewd women" that accompanied their presence.

In 1924, the Immigration Act made official the Marfa Sector, which paved the road for the present-day presence of US Customs and Border Protection (CBP). In 2011, the Marfa Sector of the CBP changed its name to the Big Bend Sector. Its headquarters remains in Marfa, although it was headquartered in next-door Alpine in the 1930s and '40s. The Big Bend Sector is the largest station of the Border Patrol, spanning 135,000 square miles and 510 border miles.[36] About seven hundred Border Patrol agents work in the Big Bend Sector, with about seventy-five working in and around Marfa. The headquarters also employs about fifty civilian employees and twenty officers, and half of its employees are of Hispanic descent.[37]

In 1931, the War Department recommended the abandonment of Fort D. A. Russell, and in 1933 the long-standing cavalry troops were transferred to Fort Knox, Kentucky, and switched from horses to automobiles. The Claes Oldenburg and Coosje van Bruggen piece at the Chinati Foundation, *Monument to the Last Horse*, is a memorial to one ill-fated horse of the cavalry. Called Old Louie, he was too old to be transferred to another post when the horses were redistributed. As the story goes, Louie was draped in black, killed (one can only hope it was a quick and painless death), and buried on the grounds. *Monument* is an oversized horseshoe with its U turned downward, and it is installed between two bunkers at Chinati. When the artists had their time in residence at Chinati in 1987, many relics from Fort D. A. Russell's heyday were scattered on the property, and it is these nails and horseshoes that inspired them.

The fort was reopened in 1935, after being reconsidered as a strategic location for protection of the border, and Works Progress Administration (WPA) funding enabled some improvements and additional buildings. Improvements funded by the Highway Acts of 1921 and 1956[38] helped create better roads and easier access from Marfa to Presidio to the south, Alpine to the east, Fort Davis to the north, and El Paso to the west. The cattle, wool, mohair, and cotton industries did well during the middle of the twentieth century, and for a time the silver industry also did well with the Shafter mine, which closed and reopened with some regularity before closing for good in 1942, at which point Shafter turned into a ghost town. Amazingly, the Shafter mine reopened in 2012, reviving the ghost town—if only temporarily.[39]

With Marfa's population growing, the Hotel Paisano opened in 1930 in anticipation of an oil boom that never came. Eventually falling into disrepair, it was saved in 2001 by investors who purchased the hotel for $185,000 (the amount owed on back taxes)[40] at auction on the courthouse lawn. The hotel was renovated to its original charm and is now on the National Register of Historic Places, one of four such sites in Marfa.[41] The hotel's outdoor courtyard is one of the most popular gathering spots for both locals and tourists, and the lobby's leather seating and darkly stained wood pair well with the large buffalo and Hereford heads mounted across from the front desk.

A United Service Organizations (USO) building constructed in Marfa during World War I today serves as the Marfa Visitor Center and can be rented out for weddings or even film shoots. While improvements have been made to the exterior walls and lobby, the grand central space looks much as it did originally and holds quite a bit of nostalgia. In the 1970s, a former soldier had the idea of posting photos of all the military soldiers from the Marfa area on the walls of the large dance hall. The result is a series of grids with black-and-white 8 × 10 photographs of soldiers, spanning nearly the entire life of the military in West Texas. The chandelier is a replacement—the original had nearly disintegrated—and an elegant and grand centerpiece to the room.

While the USO building was being constructed, the War Department conducted surveys and research to determine if and where an airport could be built for the purposes of training pilots. In 1942, the Marfa Army Airfield was built east of town, and airplanes started arriving toward the end of the year. The fact that the railroad ran through Marfa contributed to the decision to build an airfield there, and the year-round flying conditions didn't hurt. When complete, the airfield covered 2,750 acres with nearly 250 buildings and six runways, and an additional six auxiliary runways in the surrounding area. It is a remarkable feat that the United States was able to build its World War II training airfields as quickly as it did all over the country, but no more remarkable than the airfields' almost-instantaneous closures once they were considered surplus.

The combination of men from Fort D. A. Russell and the Marfa Army Airfield ballooned the population of Marfa over the World War II years, reaching an apex of five thousand people, and servicemen and locals interacted frequently through sports, dinners, dances, and on the streets of town.[42] Overall, the people of Marfa welcomed the young men into their lives and acted as a support system while the men were far from home. In 1943, up to two hundred German prisoners of war (POWs) arrived at the fort, which served as a POW camp until the end of the war. Mostly, the Germans were well behaved, and later interviews reveal that most rather enjoyed their time in Marfa[43]—with the exception of one failed escape attempt[44]—and they mainly spent their time marching around town or maintaining the fort's property.

Interior of the USO building, 2011.

The flying school at the Marfa Army Airfield prospered during these war years. Marfa remains a spectacular location for flying, tucked into the Marfa Plateau between the surrounding mountains. Air casualties did occur regularly, but in total the base trained approximately eight thousand pilots. Like most American towns during World War II, the general social and economic focus in Marfa was on supporting the war, and all residents' lives were affected. Although the massive air base was in many respects a self-contained small town, it was not uncommon for base dwellers to travel into town for shopping and socializing. This resulted in many marriages to local girls, but a precise estimate is hard to gauge.

Following the end of World War II in 1945, it was recommended that both the Marfa Army Airfield and Fort D. A. Russell go into inactive status; the airbase closed the following year. The fort saw the last of its German POWs depart in 1945, and it never regained active status. In 1949, the fort's land was sold to private ownership. Divorced from war, Marfa's economy plummeted and would not prosper again until the artistic surge decades later. The airfield hung on, hosting a route of Trans-Texas Airways from 1948 to 1960[45] and keeping its runways operational until about the early 1980s.[46]

By then, the auxiliary fields were no longer needed, and piece by piece, the base was dismantled and its structures sold or transferred. Some buildings ended up at Sul Ross University in Alpine. Today the airfield is a hidden landscape, but its runways and flight lines remain imprinted on the earth, too stubborn to go away completely. A 2011 graduate architecture studio at Princeton University proposed ways to reuse and repurpose the space of the airfield,[47] and there was even an attempt in 2011 to transform the former runways into a car racetrack.[48] Given my unabashed obsession and fascination with the airfield, I've thought a lot about how it could be reused in an informative way that references its history. The racetrack proposal wouldn't work; Marfa is too slow-paced to handle something so hurried.

Here's what I'd do: I'd keep the fence immediately surrounding the runways but remove any interior fencing, and I'd leave all the loose hangar remnants and foundation blocks that dot the landscape. I'd leave most of the runways and ramp as is, but I would

Aerial view of the former Marfa Army Airfield, looking east, 2011.

clean up the large trees and shrubs that have overtaken the runways, to allow for both pedestrian and bike traffic. I'd take the standard runway lights that you see at any airport (white, yellow, red, orange, and blue) and install them just as if the airport were in use. Then, I'd open the gate at the entrance to the airfield and pave the road that leads down from the highway. The airfield would become a park, and at night you'd see the sparkle of all those lights close to the ground, mirroring the mystery lights that are visible from the same area. Because the lights from the airfield would interrupt the views from the Marfa Lights Viewing Center, I'd put them on a timer so that they would come on periodically throughout the evening for a short period of time (for example, at 6:00, 7:00, and 8:00 p.m. for 15-minute intervals). Finally, I'd make sure to build a path to my concrete wall, so that others could experience the changing perspective it offers.

It would be a simple, visual, and quiet way to pay homage to the history of the space without interrupting the landscape. This would make use of the space in a way similar to Tempelhof Field in the center of Berlin, a closed historic airport, or even the High Line on the west side of Manhattan, an abandoned aboveground rail line, both of which were turned into public parks in recent years. History would not be erased, but it would be changed in a way that allows new access and insight.

After the military departed, life in Marfa continued without major disruption through the last few years of the 1940s. Then, between 1950 and 1957, Texas experienced a severe drought that devastated the ranching industry.[49]

One event happened during the drought of the 1950s that still has an impact on the town to this day.[50] In 1955, the epic movie *Giant*, based on the 1952 novel by Edna Ferber, was filmed in Marfa over a handful of weeks. It was released the next year and was nominated for ten Academy Awards, and won Best Director for George Stevens. This film is especially interesting as a case study for film tourism because it shows how a major movie production can be a gift to the community that keeps on giving.[51] *Children of Giant*, from 2015, is a documentary about the making of the film that focuses on the experience of the Hispanics in Marfa, as extras and as part of a segregated community.

While ranchers were used to having good and bad years as measured by rainfall, this drought simply didn't break for seven full years. Ranchers were forced to sell off their cattle or buy feed to maintain them, adding a major expense. As one local rancher described the drought, "You have to cut your cows because you don't have enough to feed them. The revenue is cut, but the needs are constant, so you just hope for a better day." Another said, "There's not much to say about a drought. You look to the sky and pray for rain."

Rain finally came in 1957, enough to officially end the drought and bring renewed hope to the ranchers. However, Marfa had already been affected and was losing some of its population. In 1940, the town's population was 5,000, and by 1950, that number had dropped to 3,603. Stores had closed, and folks had already moved elsewhere in search of work.

While the concept of environmental determinism has long been out of vogue, when I look at the climate and geology and general environment of Marfa and Presidio County, I have to wonder how you can *avoid* having your way of life influenced by these things. Largely uncontrollable, they are some of the most dominant forces of the area. People in the area have a certain resolve to keep life going, regardless of what the land might otherwise indicate. The land, as I sometimes need to remind myself, doesn't care about me. Any value or beauty that I might see in the land is my own doing, nothing more.

While the *idea* of the rancher is still alive in Marfa, ranching no longer appears to be the exclusive way of life for most. Every rancher I know in Marfa has another job, one that puts food on the table, fills the tank with fuel, and keeps the electricity running. Yet ranching remains an important part of Marfa's culture and identity.

I'd been desperate to learn more about the complexities of ranching in West Texas. I knew that there was a lot I didn't know, and I also wanted to get past my own bias against ranching. It can't be denied that the land has changed at the hands of humans and their industries. As one scholar wrote of the effects of ranching in

West Texas, "An entire biological community that had taken millennia to evolve was destroyed in less than a quarter of one century,"[52] referring to the end of the nineteenth century. Although I had had some very nice chats with ranchers over several years, I got the sense that I was always being told what I wanted to hear or that I just wasn't being told the whole truth.

For example, one local rancher told me that he only really ranched cattle anymore because it was what he knew; that he didn't keep many cows, and that it was more a hobby than anything else. I relayed this remark to another rancher, who told me that I had better believe this man was making money off of his cows and that no one is ranching as a hobby. Had I been duped? Yes and no, I imagine. I think ranchers do enjoy the work they do, and I think part of it may certainly be because of familial history and their enjoyment of working the land. But the more I got to know about the industry, the more I realized that making money was always going to be the main consideration.

I enlisted a friend in town to help me meet some more ranchers. After a few false starts (ranchers do not want to talk to outsiders), I was finally able to sit down with a longtime Marfan and rancher. When I arrived at his house, I saw a tall, slender white man wearing a wide-brimmed hat, standing outside speaking to a Hispanic worker about a large gasket, which presumably belonged to one of the many trucks parked on the street. He invited me inside and gave me a glass of water.

"Well now, what do you want to talk about?"

I said I wanted to better understand ranching.

"Well, the environment is so dynamic that it is really hard to summarize it."

I asked him to walk me through what he knew. To start, I wanted to know more about him and his time in Marfa.

How long have you lived in Marfa? (44 years.) Why did you come here? (I got a job on a ranch.) What has been the greatest change you have seen? (The people.) Did you know Donald Judd? (Yes.) Was he nice? (I don't know if I'd call him *nice*, but he was always pleasant.) How would you characterize the relationship between Anglos and Mexicans? (It's very complicated when you try to discuss it.) Have you toured Chinati? (Once, a long time ago. I didn't go back.) Would you agree that Marfa has settled into an identity as a tourist town? (Probably.) What do you do in your free time? (I don't have any.)

He pointed out something that had not occurred to me, and yet seemed obvious after he had said it. I had asked him how many severe droughts he had seen during his many years in Marfa.

"Well, maybe three or four, but again, that is a difficult question to answer." The rancher used the word "spotty" to describe Marfa's rainfall. Rain is unpredictable. Even an intense storm over a given period of time might bring rain to some areas and not others. It may rain all over one ranch and barely touch the one next door. The only thing that breaks that pattern is a hurricane in the Gulf of Mexico, which causes rain in the desert, which in turn allows the subsoil to improve and get more moisture, bringing the creeks to life with weeds and other plants, which ultimately equals food for the cattle. Ranching is dependent on water, but water is not necessarily going to land where you want it to.

"The climate is overrated. The wind never stops. You can't stay out in the sun for very long at this altitude because you will just burn up," the rancher says. He's absolutely right, I think. When in Marfa, I'm always driving. On the rare occasion that I walk somewhere, the sun allows for no escape. At the edge of town, with no protection from any structures, the wind seems never to stop. But this isn't a new component to the area's identity. The wind of West Texas was treated as a character in Dorothy Scarborough's *The Wind*, from 1925, based in Sweetwater, Texas (a mere 300 miles from Marfa). The wind will drive a person mad, as it does to the book's main character. The intense and palpable swirl of a strong wind can be terrifying.

Ranching is an extremely complicated business—this I am told again and again. The income varies. Operations are different. Taxes have to be paid. Investments have to be paid for. Experts in the field can disagree on almost anything. There are different operators, different objectives, different techniques employed, differences in the education of all parties, and perhaps the worst of all, in the opinions of all parties.

One of the first ranchers in the area, Lucas (Luke) Brite, wrote an essay at some point before his death in 1941 reflecting on his life of ranching and his arrival to West Texas:

> The beautiful valleys bordered by mountains were untouched by man. As far as we know this spot had been in waiting since the dawn of creation for development that it might contribute to the support and dominion of man.[53]

Brite's estate would eventually span 125,000 acres of land for his Hereford cattle (no. 88 on the list of the 100 largest landowners in the United States; Brad Kelley, who also owns land in West Texas, including the land on which the army airfield sits, is no. 4 with 1,500,000 acres),[54] and the estate is still managed today by his heirs.[55] But as these historic ranches have aged, the next generations don't always agree on how each operation should run. It's the "100-year rule" as described by one rancher—after one hundred years, the ranch gets too big for itself; things start to break down, and families squabble. Even when the land is sold to new owners, not all of them use it to farm or ranch—at least not as they did in the past. That means there just isn't the same return on investment on the land as there was a few decades ago.

Indeed, not all landowners are motivated by possible monetary returns on the land. One day I spent part of an afternoon at the Dixon Water Foundation, whose mission is to "promote healthy watersheds through sustainable land management to ensure that future generations have the water resources they need."[56] Dixon is largely a research and demonstration ranch, but they do breed cattle and sell their calves every two years.

I met up with Robert, the president and CEO, to talk about ranching and to see the property, in the Dixon Water Foundation's headquarters in a nondescript old home at the end of North Austin Street.

I ask him about tapping into the tourism industry in Marfa and how Dixon could benefit from promoting its operation by opening it up to visitors. I feel like an idiot when he points to the fence door at the edge of the ranch and the sign that says "Overlook Trail."

Perfectly timed, two people are walking by, finishing a hike on the trail. The road is open to the public during daylight hours, he says, for the very reason I've asked him about. I think how important it is to give visitors to Marfa the opportunity to get out into the land, and I'm embarrassed that I haven't already taken a walk on the Overlook Trail, that I didn't even know it was there. Maybe he does need to do a better job of promoting it.

Mimms Ranch, the site of Dixon's work, is 11,000 acres divided neatly into thirty paddocks using electric fence, most of it moveable. Two hundred head of cattle are rotated daily throughout the paddocks, but there is also a larger paddock on the northwestern part of the ranch where cattle are not moved on a regular basis. Additionally, some scattered one-acre plots of land are fenced off to keep the cattle out. These plots serve as controls to compare with the rotational and continuous grazing areas. On this ranch, two hundred head of cattle works out to about one head for every fifty acres. I ask Robert what number is standard, and unsurprisingly he tells me that it depends on a lot of factors, but largely on water and, by way of that, grass. In North Texas, where the Dixon Water Foundation has another ranch, one head to ten acres is a good ratio, but there is a lot more water there.

We leave the house and get into Robert's truck and drive up the road, heading north. Before we have gone a mile, he stops to point out a pronghorn mother who has just given birth to two calves. He hands me the binoculars and I look at the mother looking in our direction, protective and watchful. It's a perfect moment.

We continue up the road to "Joey's bench," as he calls it (designed by the local furniture maker and builder Joey Benton), which is a large round concrete seating area for trailblazers, with narrow openings at the northern and southern points so that you can enter the circle to sit down. It looks exactly like a water trough, and in this way fits right into the landscape. I also can't help but notice how Judd-like it is. We're standing at a perfect elevation to see mountains, town, and the rest of the ranch. Flies buzz around as we talk further.

I ask Robert about what happens when nothing is done to the land.

"Joey's bench" at Mimms Ranch, 2016.

"Grass can go rancid. Grass *needs* disturbance. And here, in dry and hot Far West Texas, there's less natural disturbance than in a wet climate.

"Cattle are not your enemy." That's the first thing that Dixon wants to impart to the public, he says. The second thing is that in a hot and dry climate like Marfa, there are ways to maximize the production of grass while being environmentally sound.

I understand what he is saying, and even though it makes complete sense to me, I can't help thinking of this land as "el despoblado." So much of its history has been defined by the lack of people, meaning the lack of any sort of early range management. It wasn't until the early ranchers arrived in the late nineteenth century that the land was used in any substantial grazing capacity outside of native animals roaming free. And these early people made lots of money off of it. With this money, they built the downtown infrastructure. And they spent it on beautiful homes that still stand in Marfa.

One of these homes, the Brite mansion, is spectacular. Nearly everything in the home is original, from the geometric inlays in the hardwood floors of the dining room to the cedar-lined closets in the bedrooms. The teal and robin's-egg-blue walls are charming and whimsical, and the sofas in the living room nearly swallow you up. The office has a beautiful roll-top desk and simple pen and watercolor landscape drawings of the ranch and its cattle. Although the Brite family continues to ranch the land, the house itself is a beautiful relic of an era long gone.

On May 20, 1997, a young boy who had just turned eighteen was tending to his family's goats in Redford, Texas—a tiny border town about ninety minutes from Marfa and thirty minutes from Presidio—when he was shot and killed by a four-member unit of the Marines that was training in the area. The Marines say that they mistook him for a drug runner. This young man was the first American to be killed on native soil by US military forces since the 1970 Kent State shootings.[57]

The teenager, Esequiel Hernández Jr., was armed with a .22 rifle, not an uncommon accessory for a rancher in West Texas to carry. The four Marines were from Joint Task Force Six, a unit that assists state and local law enforcement agencies in counter-drug operations.[58] The unit was in the area working with the Border Patrol on a joint drug trafficking venture, but its members were not properly trained about the customs and habits of the area residents (such as the normalcy of being armed when goat herding in West Texas). Further, the Redford community had not been notified that armed Marines were going to be training in the area. This combined lack of education and information is credited with causing the tragedy, but during the investigation, conflicting reports placed blame on either party. Some of the Marines accused the boy of firing shots toward them, while others in the unit maintained that the boy had never seen them.[59] The complications that arose from these conflicting reports brought a lot of political attention to the Border Patrol and its policies, and Hernández's killing started a nationwide discussion about the border that continues today.

Marfa's proximity to the border raises the question: Can the geography of Marfa and the border define its people? Marfa is not a border town in the strictest sense of the term—it's not located at the border to Mexico like Presidio is—but its location one hour from the US-Mexico border places it within the framework of borderland culture, politics, and economy, and the combination of these qualities and its geography is often referred to as "the border." The border is almost its own country, a blend of both Mexico and the United States. The increase in Border Patrol agents and activity in recent years has made the area particularly militarized, and some have described the border as a "scene of an ongoing economic conquest."[60] The Redford killing is a devastating consequence of this militarization.

The Big Bend Sector of the US Customs and Border Protection is an entirely different place when compared to other areas along the border with Mexico. It is the largest sector, and the landscape is the most rugged. "This country is desolate, and it's full of old-time Texans, and on both sides of the river people are real independent," says a Border Patrol agent.[61] It is the most challenging area to cross for anyone trying to illegally come into the United States from Mexico. The surrounding mountains create barriers that are nearly impossible to traverse, and the sun and heat are tough to battle even in the best conditions. Finding yourself without water or food is death. Many ranchers will leave jugs of water throughout their land so that they don't later find bodies, dead from dehydration. The Border Patrol has seen a rise in both drug trafficking and illegal crossings,[62] which has contributed to the growth of the Big Bend Sector's personnel. Despite this growth, only 10 percent of the Big Bend Sector remains in "operational control" due to the forbidding landscape.[63] In essence, there is a lot of landscape out there to contend with, and both the Border Patrol and the inhabitants of West Texas are at its mercy.

From the border town of Lajitas, there's a winding, meandering road that runs parallel to the Rio Grande. I spent a long and lazy Sunday driving from Marfa east to Marathon, then south down to Big Bend, eventually turning west toward Terlingua, dipping southwest to Lajitas, and, following this road up to Redford and Presidio, finally back to Marfa. The dry and brown-beige cliffs at eye level and above meet a sharp contrast when hitting the water line of the river. Lush, verdant large trees reach up out of the green-blue water. Kayaking and fishing are common activities, and if the heat and sun call for it, a dip in the water is satisfying and refreshing. Within Big Bend National Park, you can even cross over to Boquillas, Mexico, for tacos and enchiladas.

How strange that just on the other side of the river is another country. The flowy, curvy, and peaceful body of water separates two nations, but judging from the geology and topography on either of its sides, the landscape appears as one.

Periodically, massive marijuana caches are found at the highway checkpoint between Presidio and Marfa, and this keeps the area Border Patrol on constant alert. Consequently, Marfa's residents must live alongside an inherently mistrustful organization. The Border Patrol's jurisdiction stretches for hundreds of miles along the Big Bend Sector, and this, along with the uptick in crime, has necessitated a steady increase in agents. Between 1993 and 2012, the agent staffing increased from 3,444 to 18,546 in the Southwest sectors, of which the Big Bend is a part.[64] Back in the 1990s, the

Border Patrol simply didn't have sufficient human power, which is how the US Marines became involved via Joint Task Force-Six (which was renamed Joint Task Force-North in 2004). After the Redford killing, policy changed, and although the military has since returned in recent years to assist the Border Patrol, their members now do so unarmed. As for the marine who shot and killed Hernández, he was acquitted of charges of murder.

I think about Marfa's placement near the border and what that has meant for its residents. Not only does the community grapple with the Border Patrol's mission of combating drugs and illegal immigrants, it also must deal with the challenges of its growing tourism economy against the backdrop of its history and demographics. Marfa's population in 2016 is 69 percent Hispanic and has more or less always been this way.[65] Specifically, of its 1,981 residents (from the 2010 census), 1,360 are of Hispanic origin, with the remaining 621 not of Hispanic origin. Put another way, 1,782 are white alone, 136 are some other race alone, 38 are two or more races, 12 are black or African American alone, 12 are American Indian or Alaska native alone, and 1 is Asian alone. So, when I speak of Anglos and Hispanics in Marfa, I am speaking about most of the population.

How do you quantify discrimination? How do you measure what so often goes unsaid, and is taboo, and is swept under the rug? One Marfa native, Tony Cano, took on the task in writing a memoir of growing up in Marfa, living south of the railroad tracks, where "his" kind belonged.[66] As a kid, he defiantly walked into Marfa Elementary to enroll there instead of at the Blackwell School, which until its 1965 closing was a segregated school for Hispanic students. His thoughtful portrayal of Marfa during the 1950s is evidence of a divided town but also of a town that was changing. He and his friends make the varsity football team while the white kids do not, and he and his friends have adventures with the "forbidden" white girls of their age who see past race but who must go against their parents' disapproval. For that era in Marfa, and certainly in the rest of the country, discrimination was a way of life, and the older generations weren't ready to let it go.

When the Blackwell School closed in January 1965,[67] the Marfa Elementary absorbed its students. Some Hispanic residents remember having to carry their desks from their old school to their new one, which they took as evidence of an unwelcoming community. But I don't believe this was intended to ostracize these students. I spoke with the former principal of Marfa Elementary, who also recalled the day the schools integrated. When I mentioned the Blackwell students having to carry their desks across town, he said that the story was "inaccurate." It was a hectic day to be sure, and various custodians and teachers were helping the little ones get settled. Still, multiple recollections by Hispanic residents very clearly recall that day, and having to carry their desks, and of feeling unwelcome in the new school. Each student from that time can probably recount his or her own personal experience of what it felt like, either as a white or a Hispanic person.

Even before Blackwell's closure, the students were not allowed to speak Spanish at school. One teacher thought up a burial ceremony in 1954, wherein the students symbolically "buried" their native tongue, referring to it as "Mr. Spanish."[68]

Marfa may in some ways remain divided by race, but what town can boast a lack of discrimination?

"Friction between Marfa's communities is minimal," says one resident.[69]

What is most telling to me, as an outsider looking at Marfa, is the fact that the cemeteries remain segregated by a fence, dividing white from Hispanic. For all that locals can say about the feeling of camaraderie in Marfa, there remains an elephant in the room: the damn fence. There has been no discussion about the fence in the newspaper or through a public forum, although the Merced Cemetery—part of the Hispanic side—did receive the gift of an additional acre of land from the heirs to the previously named Brite Ranch. This allowed native Hispanics to continue to be buried in Marfa (as their cemetery became full in 2008), but it doesn't solve the problem of the fence. One Marfa native, a Hispanic man, relayed to me a sentiment from an old native white rancher: "As long as I am alive, that fence will not be taken down." Tick tock.

Cemeteries have always fascinated me. When I visit my mother's grave in Hanover, Pennsylvania, I sit at her headstone and think of what state of decay her body is in (Is there skin left? Have the maggots gone? Are her clothes still there?), a mere six feet below me. I remember learning about the Zoroastrian burial tradition when I was in high school. Zoroastrians put the bodies of their deceased outside, on a "Tower of Silence," where they are left exposed to birds. I think this is the noblest way to be transferred back to nature. In Marfa, however, the dead are buried in the cemeteries, and I decided to map it.

I was inspired by the 2010 Denis Wood book, *Everything Sings*. The book is a compilation of dozens of maps of one neighborhood, Boylan Heights, in Raleigh, North Carolina. Each map looks at something incredibly specific—the location of wind chimes, where the jack-o-lanterns are placed come Halloween, what the local rents are—and the result is an intensive and strangely beautiful compilation of the markings of this one small community. In Marfa, I started with the cemeteries: where the headstones are, what the names are, where the trees are, where the fences are.

There are three cemeteries in Marfa: the Marfa Cemetery (for the whites), the Merced Cemetery (for the Hispanics), and the Catholic Cemetery (also for the Hispanics). I've gone through each row, photographed each rectangular plot, and noted each name. The Hispanic plots are the most colorful, with plastic flowers, laminated photos, and other ephemera periodically left by family members. Cars are in and out of the Merced and Catholic Cemeteries all day, every day. The Marfa Cemetery is the dullest, and I have seen few cars and visitors there. There is very little color, but given that whites don't celebrate the dead like Mexicans do, it's not very surprising to see these differences. When finished, my map of the Marfa Cemetery will be a subjective, anthropological picture of the literal components of this space. And the location of the fences, the division of Hispanic from Anglo names, will also, I hope, be telling. Maybe it will inspire people to go into the cemetery in the middle of the night and pull up all the fences.

Because Marfa has a largely Hispanic population, it may be reasonable to think that this culture, rather than a primarily art-focused one, would be at the forefront of Marfa's identity. In fact, many businesses are owned by Hispanics, and there is an equal Hispanic representation on the city council.[70] Discrimination has not been erased since the tumultuous times in the 1950s and 1960s, but it has waned. In speaking with various residents of Marfa, both white and Hispanic, I've actually heard more about discrimination against whites than against Hispanics. I don't know how to resolve this in my thinking. The fact that I'm white puts me in a tough spot. (Are whites just more forthcoming with me?) There's an obvious and immediate barrier between me and the Hispanics in town: I'm Other.

One retired educator who also coached high school tennis was accused of discrimination because he coached only white students. However, as he explained to me, it's not like he could force the Hispanic kids to play tennis if they didn't want to play tennis. Another native Marfan spoke about discrimination within the Hispanic community, saying that if a person is "pro-Gringo,"[71] they are treated differently. I wish I could say more about this, but I don't know where to start. This has and continues to be a void in my research on Marfa, because I'm obviously white (pale, freckled, blue-eyed), and I don't speak Spanish. Simply put, it's hard for me to access that space, which makes me feel like a terrible researcher. That said, based on my observations and interactions in town, much of any divide in the community comes down to race and other equally large factors: class, education, and culture.

And religion. One day I stepped into St. Mary's Catholic Church to attend 10 a.m. Mass, the first time I have gone to Mass in nearly twenty years. A fair number of people were in attendance, as it was the First Communion for some of the church's younger members. The little girls were adorable in their white dresses, and the young boys looked austere in their dark slacks and crisp white shirts. All of these children and the rest of the attendants were Hispanic, although a handful of white patrons were seated toward the front of the church. I felt neither welcomed nor ostracized. I was an atheist in a room full of God-fearing Catholics. I've noticed that two things bring people in Marfa together: religion and sports. If you have a child on the football team, it doesn't matter that you work at the Border Patrol or the tomato farm or the radio station. And if you go to the same church, then you're part of that same community.

Being inclusive is what most of Marfa's structured events are all about. The various cultural foundations in Marfa constantly create opportunities for local residents to partake in events. Ballroom Marfa holds a free DJ Camp each summer, for example, and the Chinati Foundation regularly offers free art classes, nature walks, and an annual Community Day to partner with and celebrate their neighbors in Marfa. The Blackwell School Alliance partners with the Chinati Foundation annually to celebrate Día de los Muertos. These types of events are geared toward all members of Marfa, not just the art-inclined ones. But as Cecilia Thompson noted, the Hispanic community does not always engage with the art one.

Still, some locals question: If Chinati or any other organization in Marfa goes out of its way to be inclusive, does it matter? If you simply don't consider the Chinati stuff art, then why should you give a damn about some open house or community day? Maybe that doesn't even matter if the result is the same. As long as the community is creating opportunities for mutual engagement, people will benefit, and ongoing dialogues can occur.

Marfa's geography makes it part of the border culture, and this in turn has impacted the culture of its residents. Over time, the culture of Marfa has become more linked to its territory, and in this way the place of Marfa is dependent on both geography and its people and culture. Through the work of its residents, foundations, and visitors, Marfa's identity can to some extent be protected while it still undergoes change, or progress. Marfa's geography isn't going to change, and thus the Border Patrol will continue to have a presence here, the current iteration of the area's long-standing military history that has shaped its culture.

Often when I've spoken to someone unfamiliar with Marfa, I've gotten this response: "Martha?"

"No, Marfa."

"Mar-FUH?"

"Marfa. Yes."

"MAR-FUH. Huh."

"Yes."

The source of Marfa's name is a debated topic, and although it seems like a small matter, the details hold a larger significance for Marfa's cultural identity.

I am sitting at the bar in the beer garden one lazy afternoon when I overhear an older white-haired man from out of town ask the person next to him if she is from Marfa. She is.

"Why is it called Marfa?"

"I don't know."

"I can answer that," I respond, uninvited. They both look at me with interest.

"Well, for years it was said that Marfa was named after a character in a Dostoyevsky novel."

Now they look at me with blank stares. I continue, undeterred.

"But a few years back, another researcher determined that it was in fact named after a character in a book called *Michael Strogoff*."

More blank stares.

"Which is a book and then a play by Jules Verne."

The out-of-towner recognizes that name.

"Jules Verne?"

"Yes, this researcher, Barry Popik, concluded that Marfa was a character in the book and play *Michael Strogoff* by Jules Verne."

The local tells us, "I've lived here my whole life and I had no idea."

Dostoyevsky's *Crime and Punishment* has been named as the source of Marfa's name for reasons unclear.[72] That Dostoyevsky used the name Marfa for nine different characters in six novels is no help in narrowing down a source text.[73] Most writings on Marfa accepted that *The Brothers Karamazov* was the source, despite some questions about the theory's plausibility—not to mention the earlier sources that point to *Michael Strogoff* as well as the Russian novella *Marfa Posadnitsa*.[74]

When the train was being run through Marfa in the early 1880s, the railroad executive's wife, Hanna Maria Strobridge, was the one to name the town, as she did others along the railroad's path. A woman in her position would have been well educated and well traveled, so it is no surprise that she would have been reading various now-classic texts. Other towns in Texas share the literary-character theme, including Longfellow, Emerson, Dryden, and Marathon.[75]

Some researchers[76] and others have made the point that, as *The Brothers Karamazov* was published in December 1880,[77] and Marfa was named on January 16, 1882, it was highly unlikely that Strobridge would have been reading a translated novel thirteen months after its original publication.

Still, one scholar[78] suggests that there is sufficient evidence to prove that Strobridge had in fact been reading *The Brothers Karamazov* in the original Russian, and his research takes us on a path through Russian literature and language. His thesis argues that because a nearby Texas town was named Feodora and not Feodor (the important *a* suggesting that the source is Russian and not an American translation, which would have dropped the *a*), the sourcing text would have also been in Russian.

Ultimately, it is Galveston's *Daily News* of December 17, 1882, that may clarify the naming of Marfa:

> The fort [Fort Davis] is twenty-two miles north of the Southern Pacific Railroad. The nearest station is at Marfa, so named after one of the characters in the play of Michael Strogoff, and two or three other stations derive their names from Jules Verne's story.[79]

I'll go with the earliest source to conclude that Marfa was in fact named for a character in Jules Verne's *Michael Strogoff* and not Dostoyevsky's *The Brothers Karamazov*, although I know that future writing on Marfa will mention one or both.

What is important about this mystery is that for those who believe Strobridge was reading her novel in Russian, Marfa's position in history as a cultural center has been in place well before

Donald Judd, regardless of which book the name Marfa was taken from. In fact, in 1925, the Davis Mountain Federation of Women's Clubs attempted to create a Southwestern Art Center in the Davis Mountains,[80] which are located just north of Marfa, and from 1921 to 1950 there was a highly regarded art department at Sul Ross University (referred to as "The Lost Colony") that supported and educated regional painters.[81] The people of Marfa, it has been suggested,[82] have always been interested in the arts, as demonstrated by the many former venues and organizations that promoted theater, opera, dancing, and other artistic expressions. To speak of Marfa as an arts mecca, then, is not to reference only Donald Judd but instead the town's entire history, spanning back to its prominent ranching days. While Judd may prompt one to take the direct leap, nevertheless it is interesting to look back on the long influence of the arts in Marfa.[83]

An 1897 *New Era* article touted the virtues of Marfa, no doubt trying to lure transplants.[84] I think only one thing still applies:

Why come to this country?
Because the climate is perfect.
Because the soil is perfect and prolific.
Because the land is abundant and cheap.
Because a home can be made with little labor.
Because life is a luxury in a land where the sun shines
    every day.
Because there are chances for a poor man which he never
    can hope to find in older countries.
Because the country is advancing and property values are
    increasing.
Because the vast and varied resources of the country are yet
    to be developed.
Because good land is becoming more scarce, and if you don't
    catch on now, your last chance will soon be gone.
Because the worker receives a fair compensation for his labor,
    and the "rustler" has a field for the display of his energy
    and enterprise.

Because the wealth of grazing lands will soon build up a
   great and prosperous country.
Because the settler need not spend a life time in felling trees
   and grubbing out stumps.

Marfa: "Because life is a luxury in a land where the sun shines every
day."

CHAPTER 3

ENCOUNTERING THE LANDSCAPE OF MARFA

☐

I'm back at the bar of the beer garden, where I usually spend a couple of hours most weekends, on a lazy Saturday when I should be working. When I walked in a minute ago, I overheard a young hipster woman, standing in the doorway with her two hipster friends, lamenting that "Marfa kind of sucks . . . so far." The comment perked up my ears and put me on the defensive, but I was too shy to stop and ask her why she felt that way.

Halfway through my lager, the group, now four, walks up to the bar and orders a round. After paying, they make their way into the small school bus parked in a corner of the bar, repurposed as a strange and secluded seating area. I have to know what their story is—what has happened that has made them dislike Marfa—so I gather my courage, ask the gentleman beside me to watch my bag and beer for a minute, and walk up the steps of the bus.

"Excuse me," I start, "I'm so sorry to bother you all, but I believe I overheard you a few minutes ago saying that Marfa sucks, and I've been doing research here for a while, and I was just wondering what happened that made you think that?"

The one who said it—the tallest one, skinny with blond hair—is surprisingly embarrassed that I've overheard her, and she apologizes. "I'm sorry, it's just that we were down in Big Bend, and drove up today from Terlingua, and we're starving and nothing is open, and Food Shark and Boyz2Men both have a two-hour wait for food."

Ah, I think to myself. They thought they were going to be able to eat anywhere, at any time, on any given day in Marfa. I try to help them out.

"Did you try Mando's? They might be open. Or Pizza Foundation?"

They look at me with blank stares, and don't seem to be particularly interested in doing too much work here. But we start talking about Marfa and I ask them what they were planning—if anything—to do in town this weekend.

"Were you planning to take a tour of Chinati?"

"Chinati?"

"The museum." More blank stares. I offer them a hint.

"Donald Judd."

"Donald who?"

It dawns on me in that instant that the new Marfa is entirely different from what it was just ten short years ago. As has become a trend, these four young travelers came to Marfa only because they had heard that it was a cool place and they wanted to check it out. But they are underwhelmed—one of them uses that word, "underwhelmed"—and I feel sorry for them. I feel sorry for all tourists everywhere, myself included, who expect so much from places while not even considering that an investment of time and research might be required of them.

"We're from Austin," another girl says. "Marfa seems like a poor man's Austin." I try to laugh at that comment, but I feel defeated, and my beer is getting warm.

Back at the bar, the guy next to me strikes up a conversation. He came to Marfa from Montana and did some construction work at the Hotel Saint George while it was being built, before getting a job shoeing horses in Alpine. He's white, and he tells me about the local pecking order for manual labor. He, like the girls, seems to be sore about his experience in Marfa.

"If you're white, you're on the bottom. Tim Crowley and Joey Benton only hire Mexican workers." I consider whether or not that's a bad thing.

Later, I ask Joey about his position. He's thoughtful about his answer, and says that he hires people who need jobs and do good work. The quality of a person, he says, has nothing to do with race.

At my perch at the bar, I'm still distracted by the girls' comments about Marfa, about how they don't get the place of Marfa. They're passing through the landscape at too fast a pace to understand any of it.

At its core, the field of geography is an exploration of landscape, space, and place, and I look at Marfa using these three terms as a structure. Seemingly interchangeable, these three words refer to nuanced translations of the environment that surrounds us and in which we move about. To a geographer, landscape is different from space, and space is different from place. I've spent nearly all of my academic life, as an anthropologist and geographer and artist, thinking about these three words, and in the past six years I've focused my lens on the small and quirky Marfa. Because the expansiveness of Marfa's geography is one of its most relished characteristics, it seems fitting to spend time breaking apart its landscape, space, and place.

The landscape of Marfa is the landscape of West Texas, in the Chihuahuan Desert. It is dry, and it is hot, and when up, the sun is unforgiving and relentless. At night, the coal-dark sky fills with so many stars that you think you can just reach your hand up to pluck one out of the air. Other times, it seems that the stars compose a thick blanket, heavy enough to sink down to the street to meet you.

Landscape is the unit concept in geography, and on its most basic level refers to the surface of the earth or part of it.[1] It is where I begin research and inquiry; it's where everything happens. It is also an ambiguous term "used by artists, earth scientists, architects, planners, historians, archaeologists, and geographers."[2] And it's a misleading concept because of its ambiguity and because it contains multiple layers of meaning; it's often viewed and discussed differently, and I am constantly trying to understand and depict it. No two persons see the same landscape, and no two social groups make precisely the same evaluation of the environment.[3] In this way the environment is a consistently fluid landscape, adjusting to the individual based on his or her memory, history, and experience. The ranchers, Hispanics, makers, retirees, and other residents of Marfa perceive and experience their landscape differently, and the tourists who come to Marfa also have their own equal but unique experience.

Looking at landscape is a learned process; to see something is both to observe and to grasp it intellectually.[4] I take the term for granted, because I can see the landscape, but I cannot see the landscape in its entirety until I have trained my eyes and my mind to notice that which is unwritten on the landscape. This looking, or seeing, is also affected by what I seek to uncover.

Landscape may be an intensely visual idea because of its historical association with art.[5] I *look at* landscape; I experience landscape; I draw it, paint it, photograph it; and it surrounds me everywhere I go. But landscape is not purely visual; it is also a constructed environment, and to say that an environment is constructed is to say that on some level, someone with power is making decisions about its construction. In this remote part of Texas, this power came with the early white ranchers and with the railroad, both of which defined the history and identity of Marfa for many years. When I speak of the term "landscape," then, I speak of a deceptively simple term that is actually quite substantive, depending on histories and perspectives as well as intentions. Landscape also exerts a subtle power over people, eliciting a broad range of emotions and meanings that may be difficult to specify.[6] I love it and I fear it, so I want to understand and control it. Our landscapes define us, but we also define our landscapes.

If culture is a set of values and behavioral patterns that are often shared within a group, then culture can be placed onto the landscape. In this way the cultural landscape is a product of both the physical world and the social world. Marfa is defined by its physical landscape, but it is also defined by its cultural offerings, which over the past twenty years have been weighted heavily toward the arts. Landscape is a series of visual expressions of material culture, and it is also something to be perceived and responded to.[7]

I've already said that Marfa is an intensely visual landscape. What I mean by this is that both its physical geography and its cultural presence are expansive. The landscape of Marfa—its dry climate, endless vistas, wide blue skies, and flat plains interrupted by jagged, barren mountain ranges—has always been written about as a character in its history. The landscape is not just a setting or background; it is also part of the story, and the story is developed in response and relation to this landscape. That the landscape is inherent to the story is not unique to Marfa; however, it seems to be particularly intense here. This is perhaps because of the intensity of the physical environment. The sun is harsh; the storms, albeit rare, are intense with hail and thunder; the lack of rain creates droughts that carry sincere threats.

Concurrently, the cultural landscape is just as intense because of the varied histories of Marfa: the ranching, the proximity to and relationship to the border, the overarching military presence, and, finally, the art. The story of Donald Judd and the last thirty years of Marfa have created a cultural intensity that goes well beyond the borders of Marfa, Presidio County, and Texas.

Landscapes affect the way I experience place, and as I get to know a landscape, I shift my perception of it; the landscape intensifies. The landscape of West Texas is the setting for the space and place of Marfa. Space and place are two sides of the same coin; one cannot exist without the other. Together, they compose a landscape.

While space is a concrete matter that can be measured, photographed, or altered, place is an intangible form that is both dependent on and complementary to the space. When I think of space, I think of area or cubic feet, or of tangible things that I can visualize in my mind if not before my eyes. Space is a setting that I can take part in, either individually or collectively, through movement and experience. Space is the background of my life and is what homes and buildings and roads are built on. I take up space by my movements and my voice. I conquer and repurpose space. I work to free some spaces and sometimes to destroy others. Space is not a given; it is constructed, literally, and this construction is dependent on social, economic, and historical factors. The physical quality of space—and even the absence of it—is a powerful component of my life. In Marfa, the qualities of space define the experience of place.

Place is lived space. Place is filled with meaning and context, and it means different things to different people. For some, the place of Marfa is home. For others, it's a destination, a scene to be seen in. This place of Marfa is specific to each individual, and place must be understood in the larger context of experience and observation. When I think about Marfa's sense of place, I think about all of its unique qualities and my personal interactions with them. I am fascinated with Marfa, as I am with many small towns, but that alone does not make Marfa a fascinating place. I am constantly reminding myself that Marfa is, despite its popularity, "just another goddamn small Texas town," to quote a professor of mine.

"I think it's a mistake to think of Marfa as a place that needs to be understood or a place that has a unique mix of this and that," a friend in Marfa tells me one night. "Because all places have that." He's right—the place of Marfa depends on the people who occupy it at any given time, and this changes with time.

The vernacular landscape can tell the story of place much better than its monuments. It is real, and functional, and without pretense. Have you ever gone to a new place and really looked at every aspect of its structure? Put yourself on assignment the next time you take a trip. It's better if you have been to the place before. What color is the sidewalk—is it made of concrete or brick? Is there graffiti anywhere—what does it say? Where is the paint peeling—from a storefront door on a main street or on the wall of a lesser-traveled alleyway? How tall is the tallest building? If you were to write in a journal, describing in detail what you saw, what would you focus on?

It's easy to take something as simple as vision for granted. I use my eyes to get from point to point. I use my eyes to see how long the wait is at the coffee shop, or to read the menu at a restaurant. I forget to notice other details, the small things that add up to compose the place. I've been looking at Marfa with intentional eyes for the past six years. The small details have all added up in my mind to become my own version of Marfa. You may see similar things, and you may notice things that I have missed.

The landscape of Marfa is composed of a multitude of physical structures and components of the vernacular, in addition to the kind of specific design and architecture heralded by critics and journals on architecture. This dichotomy of place is what makes walking through Marfa so interesting: old is juxtaposed against new, form follows function, and while there are various kinds of people that both live in and visit Marfa, the distinctions among them are not always apparent. True, there are modern and minimal homes that signify wealth, and there are dilapidated adobe homes and trailers that can signify a lack of wealth, but it is misleading to think that perceptions are anything but deceiving. Marfa's structures and homes are as diverse as its people.

Most housing consists of architecturally simple structures, worn by the climate, hiding an interior oasis for refuge from the weather. Of course, plenty of homes in Marfa are carefully maintained in their stark minimalism. The newer, updated homes with minimal design keep in line with the Judd aesthetic of Marfa, but they are not the town's standard. There's one famously expensive listing currently (still? forever?) on the market: The Barbara Hill house. In the summer of 2011, I lived one block over from this home. It's a simple, minimal white house from the outside, with a low profile at one story. According to the photos I've seen of its interior, it's a one-bedroom home with the bathtub in the middle of the bedroom. The house was a former dance hall, and after spending over one year gutting and renovating its 2,319 square feet, Ms. Hill first listed it in 2015 for the inexplicable price of $895,000 (it has since been reduced to $795,000). Hill doesn't live full-time in Marfa (she's a Houston-based interior designer), and her renovation of the home attracted a lot of attention from the design community.[8] I don't mean to pick on Ms. Hill. She's a talented designer who made something beautiful in Marfa. And, that's not even the most expensive home in Marfa, but it is these kinds of properties that continue to change the demographics and character of the town.

"Black clouds of money," is how one local described it to me. Some are drawn to the remoteness of Marfa, but also to its cultural relevance that makes the town not *that* remote.

A pair of homes sit at the southwestern corner of the courthouse square. One is white and bright and minimal, with a perfectly manicured lawn. Sometimes a single car is parked in the driveway. There is never anyone outside. The home next to it is its exact opposite: a small plot of chaos. Multiple cars are parked in front on the street, and there are always children playing or adults sitting on the front porch. There's a slow cooker, a swing set, tools, bikes, and a whole lot of other stuff just—everywhere. To me, these two homes, next to each other and yet so distant aesthetically, epitomize Marfa. It's the mix of the pristine and the chaotic; the minimalism as forever influenced by Judd and the original, historic Marfa that predates him.

To experience the varying architectural diversity of one-hundred-plus years of housing, taking a walk before dawn or after dusk provides the most comfortable setting. Each road seems to have its own personality, and home styles offer a great deal of diversity: adobe, brick, concrete, prefab, mobile home, corrugated siding, corrugated fencing, wood fencing, iron fencing, no fencing. Adobe, composed of native materials, was the primary building material until after World War II. The bricks were often made directly at the building site. On some of the crumbling walls, I can see fragments of ceramic and bone, signifying the use of whatever material was lying around at the time of construction. Many people who build homes in and around Marfa tend to love adobe, but I don't understand why; it starts to deteriorate almost immediately.

White homes, blue homes, beige homes, sea green homes, gray homes. Some historic ranching homes on the upper west quadrant of town often feature some form of Mediterranean or Spanish influence, but many homes lack a definitive style, instead taking portions of a craftsman or federal design. The wrap porch is

Chaos and minimalism in Marfa, 2016.

a visual delight, stone veneer hides its true construction, and the brick homes seem heavy for this climate.

The roofs are shed, hip, and gable—the wood often begging for replacement. Metal can be a sensible choice, and unless painted, sharply reflects sunlight. When it rains on a metal roof that has not been insulated from the rest of the house, the sound from inside is amazingly loud, and terrifying.

In the yards: tires, plastic trash bins, children's toys, lawn ornaments, bicycles (always unlocked), planters, rocks stacked with intention, bird feeders, wine and beer bottles artfully placed as if sculpture, tumbleweeds. Bull skulls on posts. "Peace on earth" reads one sign.

Dogs barking, dogs barking, dogs barking.

Rogue bunnies hop around the streets and yards.

"For sale" signs are everywhere.

It is not uncommon to pass a horse and rider.

There are really good rains in the summer. I put whatever I am working on aside and move a chair to the screen door and listen. The smell of rain in Marfa is intoxicating, reminding me of my childhood and the summer rains in Virginia, and I watch the dark, heavy clouds slowly roll in from the mountains. Often, the clouds hold at the edge of town as if both threatening and tempting you, and then quickly the storm moves elsewhere.

Trees provide shade to the homes. From the air, Marfa's heavy growth of oak delineates it from the surrounding desert landscape. Some yards are more or less composed of dirt, some are carefully watered and mowed grass, but most are some mixture of the two. Trying to keep a healthy green lawn is to fight a losing battle with nature. Xeriscaping of pebbles, stones, rocks, combined with the cacti common in the Southwest, forms the landscape. One house on the northwest side of town is made of red brick and has a perfectly green lawn in the summer. I don't like this house. All I think about when I look at it is water, and the lack of it.

The edges of town offer extraordinary views of the surrounding terrain that slowly and eventually leads up to a mountain. There are the Davis Mountains to the north, the Cretaceous flats to the southeast, the Bofecillos Mountains to the south, the Chinati

Mountains to the southwest, the Sierra Vieja to the west, and the Van Horn Mountains to the northwest.[9] Marfa is semiprotected in the basin between all of this at an elevation of 4,688 feet above sea level. These mountains reveal the history of the landscape and its uses; trails have been worn into the earth, mapping physically where cultures and people have passed through. First came the Apaches, then cattlemen, then Prohibition smugglers, then Mexican immigrants and the Border Patrol.

Marfa's main drag—South Highland Avenue—and nearly every street on the grid is noticeably wider than average city streets, a quality that enhances the space: it's hard to feel physically claustrophobic in Marfa. While most homes in town have a modest or near-modest footprint in terms of yard space, those on the edge of town visually seem to expand out into the vastness of the surrounding ranchland. Despite the fact that barking dogs, passing trains, and industrial semis periodically break the silence, an overarching abundance of quietude remains throughout town.

The revealing visual qualities of the landscape change depending on how I approach Marfa. From Fort Davis to the north, I pass the Marfa Municipal Airport (formerly an auxiliary field to the Army Airfield) and the Village Farms tomato farm, both located just off the highway and adjacent to each other. Once I enter town, I drive by a few blocks of residential housing, guided by the tall, silvery water tower, then I am directed to turn west to continue on Route 17, passing the courthouse and arriving at South Highland Avenue. If I choose to stay straight on the road instead, I will dead-end at the railroad tracks but can turn right toward South Highland. It's nearly impossible to get lost in Marfa, as almost any turn will eventually lead me to one of the two main roads.

From Valentine, to the west, and after passing *Prada Marfa* earlier, the old Stardust Hotel sign more or less marks my arrival, just past the Apache Pines RV Park. Then, the cemeteries on the north side of the road; Buns N' Roses flower shop and café; Mando's Restaurant; a drive-through liquor store; Marpho Restaurant (now closed; was the Miniature Rooster and before that, the Blue Javelina); the rock shop, Moonlight Gemstones; a Stripes gas station

The water tower, 2011.

with a Subway; Dairy Queen; Marfa Museum Thrift Store; Porter's grocery (which had been the Pueblo Market); and the refurbished Thunderbird Hotel. The vintage Holiday Inn Capri sign sometimes advertises an exhibition or wedding. There are various garages to service cars; the erstwhile late-night grilled cheese shop's new occupant, Boyz2Men; Planet Marfa (a beer garden); Livingston Insurance and Real Estate offices; St. Mary's Catholic Church; and the Marfa and Presidio County History Museum.

From Presidio and Ojinaga to the south, I pass Judd's *15 untitled works in concrete* on the west side of the highway, installed on what was once a polo field for Fort D. A. Russell. The rest of the Chinati Foundation buildings stand in the background. There is the sprawling acreage of the alternative hotel and camping space, El Cosmico, with its scattered teepees, yurts, and vintage trailers ("an important stop on the road trip of life," says the precious website); the entrance to the MacGuire Ranch (matriarch Betty MacGuire is "the richest woman in Marfa," I have been told more than once); a closed Mobil gas station; Marfa Burrito; the Marfa National Bank; and a gallery space, Exhibitions 2D.

From Alpine to the east, I pass another RV park (the Tumble In); the Riata Inn; the Dollar General; Marfa Hardware (which had been ABC Pump Hardware); The Lost Horse (which had been Ray's, and Lucy's before that); Carmen's Restaurant: closed; Borunda's Restaurant: closed; another gallery (which had been the Fieldwork Marfa office and before that, Galleri Urbane); the refurbished and pristine Indie/Jacobs Gallery; Stay Marfa (sold); Wild Woolies, whose sign is painted over, which means: closed; a small shop, now vacant (which had been Cast + Crew, and before that the Velvet Antler, and before that Fancy Pony Land); Ballroom Marfa; another Stripes, this one with a Laredo Taco Company, and as I approach the four-way blinking red light, another two gas stations; Marfa Public Radio; the gallery Marfa Contemporary; and City Hall on the corner.

Heading north from the intersection up South Highland Avenue brings me home to the main drag, as it were: more City of Marfa offices; the Hotel Saint George and Marfa Book Company to my right; the large white former hotel-converted-to-Judd-offices to my left. The simple red letters spelling "Judd" above the corner doors are the only markers of its owner. Most windows are shaded or opaque and reflective, creating an eerie world of interior space against a much brighter exterior world.

The large shade structure by the train tracks has been taken down to accommodate the new hotel, but it was where the Food Shark parked its truck most days and where the farmers' market can still be found most Saturdays year-round. North of the tracks is the Marfa Post Office; the John Chamberlain building of the Chinati Foundation, which had been the Wool & Mohair Company building; a barber shop; the *Big Bend Sentinel*'s offices; the Glascock Building, now Judd's, advertising architecture; the old Marfa National Bank Building, now Judd's; the restaurant Stellina (which had been Maiya's); the Brite Building, now the Ayn Foundation's galleries; the West Texas Utilities Building; the Masonic Building, now a gym; the historic Hotel Paisano; the Palace Theater, now occupied by the illustrator David Kimble; Eugene Binder Gallery; the Texas Theater, which had been occupied by the late historian Cecilia Thompson; and finally, leading the parade: the coral-hued courthouse.

These names (always changing) may not reveal much context until you are here, walking on the sidewalk or pavement. Every space has not been named, and I somehow feel a need to fix that, but I also feel hesitation in naming as many stores as I have. Without a doubt, some will close, and a new owner will try his or her luck at something else. Or it will remain vacant space. It's impossible to keep up with the stores in Marfa because they are constantly changing. There is only so much that this small town can take in the form of boutique restaurants and high-end retail shops. Many locals wonder exactly who is buying all of these very lovely, very expensive things for sale.

Visibly, Marfa is fairly akin to other small Texas towns. Sure, it doesn't look like much, but many of its storefronts show a careful maintenance that is evidence of its bustling, if sometimes hidden and seasonal, community. Some buildings and homes are more buttoned up than others, and it can be difficult to determine if one space is occupied and another isn't. The creative-minded owners here seem to have a special affinity for keeping the layers of paint and signage that have been worn over the years. They are visible markers of history, evidence that the past is right here with us.

The people of Marfa can be divided into various groups, but these days it truly comes down to this: the residents and the tourists. Among the residents in Marfa are further delineations: the Hispanic population, the ranchers, the artists and makers, the retirees, the young people working at the various restaurants and stores, and so on. For these residents, the place of Marfa is home, perhaps uneventful but full of the quotidian acts of an existence where one works at a job (or jobs), raises a family, maintains a home, and participates in other activities. A local may never eat at the pricey Cochineal Restaurant or see anything created by Donald Judd. A local may work at the Border Patrol and spend his day in that easily identifiable white SUV with the green bands, sitting strangely by the railroad track for hours, taking his lunch at the Stripes gas station.

For the tourist, the place of Marfa may be something to contain or capture, to experience, and then to check off a list. The world of the tourist is a specific, contained experience, and one that is very different from that of the locals. The tourist may be invested in artistic, social, musical, educational, or environmental elements, and certainly any combination of these. Granted, many tourists are self-aware and try to be good visitors. The experience of Marfa is different for me because I am an outsider, no matter how many times I come here or how much I feel I know about its people and culture. I'm a forever-tourist to Marfa, but I believe this separation helps me view its complexity and its changes.

Place in Marfa can be experienced in countless ways, based on the needs and desires of the inhabitant or visitor. It is experiential perspective,[10] where experience is the culmination of sensation, perception, and conception. What does the place of Marfa entail? It is the combination of the people who live here and those who are visiting. It is the quiet activity that occurs each weekday inside the library, or the sounds of the espresso machine inside Frama, where a two-person line constitutes a rush. It is the patio of Jett's Grill in the Hotel Paisano on an early evening, when it is cool enough to sit outside and where you are more likely to know someone there than not.

While the Chinati and Judd Foundations draw in a respectable number of visitors each year, an increasing trend in using Marfa as a destination-wedding spot is expanding the tourism industry. Intensive multiday courses in design and architecture put on by local foundations and nonprofits and multiple music and film festivals also draw visitors to the town.[11] While the tourist may come to Marfa with a specific agenda in mind, the nature of tourism, coupled with the literal smallness of the town, allows for cross-pollination of areas of interest. Someone coming to Marfa to attend a wedding may also engage in the local art scene or with nature, or perhaps take an aerial tour of the town and its surrounding geography. Because of this, it can be very difficult to accurately describe the people of Marfa and the visitors to Marfa, and it's unfair to compartmentalize both people and place. The world is diverse, even the world of a small West Texas town.

Marfa has an eerie quality throughout the daylight hours. Unless an event is happening, resulting in a surge of people to the outdoors (the parade during the annual Marfa Lights Festival, for instance), the space of Marfa is relatively quiet and absent of people. However, as a functioning town with various daily happenings—folks in and out of the post office, incoming and departing guests at the Hotel Paisano, the judge and staff of the courthouse carrying on with business—there is a regular presence that permeates this town as in any other. This is to say that, despite a general lack of crowding, Marfa is no ghost town. Windows are washed, sidewalks are swept, and buildings undergo repairs. In this way the space of Marfa is empty and alive at the same time.

A friend and her husband were passing through Marfa a few years ago on their way back to Austin. They had heard of the town, but this was their first time seeing it. It was a weekday, in the late morning, when they pulled into town and parked on South Highland just south of the courthouse. The street was empty, and there were no people around. They felt, very strongly, that they had arrived at a postapocalyptic world that may or may not contain zombies. What they experienced was entirely different from what they had imagined, based on everything they had heard about Marfa. It was an eerie experience, and they didn't particularly enjoy it. Their conception of Marfa had conflicted with the reality with which they were presented. This is a common tourist problem. It happens in Marfa because people expect a "bustling" artist community; they may even expect to be entertained. No one is going to entertain you in Marfa. Its residents will smile and engage you in conversation, perhaps, but will otherwise leave you alone. It's up to you to define what the sense of place is for you.

There's a great little text by Edward Relph, *Place and Placelessness*, which has long been out of print but continues to inspire me. I have a scanned copy that I go back to often. Relph writes that we often neither experience nor create places with more than a superficial and casual involvement,[12] and that this superficiality is what creates *placelessness*. Another term for this idea is *non-place*, where the non-place is an in-between, less valued space, and place is a positive, real space. Non-places exist because of an ever-expanding world of globalization and excess.[13]

A good example is an airport. You've neither departed from home nor arrived at a destination. The food options are probably familiar. If there is art anywhere, it's probably meant to be unobtrusive and inoffensive. The gift shops are selling the same cheap T-shirts and key chains, made in the same factory but stamped with different city names. You are constantly waiting: to check in, to get through security, to board. You're in a proverbial black hole, even though you could pull up your exact geographic coordinates on your phone. You exist, in space, in real time, but you're otherwise in a cultural dead zone. The uniformity of the experience is what can make these places seem boring or unworthy.

I've struggled with this idea because first, I love airports, and second, I'm not sure that it is philosophically possible to have a place with absolutely no meaning. One could say that the highway travel from Austin to Marfa is filled with these non-places: the gas station or Burger King off of Interstate 10, for example, whose purpose is to refuel, feed, and dismiss its patrons. If Austin (or Houston, New York, Los Angeles, Berlin, etc.) is home and Marfa is the destination, then the time filled between departing from and arriving to is ostensibly filled with wasted time and place. While Marfa has been my destination for the past six years, there is plenty of landscape, space, and place to experience on the six-hour drive from Austin. My intention, admittedly, is not to see these other sites, but I know that they are out there and worthy of my attention simply because they exist.

What's more, a place does not have to hold meaning for every individual in order to have meaning at all. An important place for me might be a placeless place for someone else. I believe the Chinati Foundation houses one of the world's finest collections of modern art, but I also know that many locals don't share this opinion. The placeless world is a world without individuality, the cause of this being technology and transportation. Speed and time have become warped, and they corrupt the ways in which we interact with our environment. But even as they rob some places of their character and meaning, they can also contribute to a place's identity, as they have allowed for Marfa's sustainability as a small and remote town. Residents of Marfa can telecommute to work, meaning they do not have to be dependent on Marfa's small economy for employment. Social media allows for the dispersion of Marfa's identity to the outside world, making it remote but not isolated.

Placelessness can have another meaning in the context of Marfa, for as Marfa is a small and remote town, it is in this way somewhat placeless in the sense that it's just another ranching town. It's just another Dairy Queen, just another Dollar General, just another block of trailer homes, and just another town where the wealthy historically have lived on one side of the tracks and the working class (in this case, Hispanics) have lived on the other. To the large portion of the population that has nothing to do with Chinati, or Judd, or any of the other foundations, it's really nothing special ("a poor man's Austin," to quote the earlier tourist). From this superficial perspective, and in these generic spaces, Marfa may be placeless as Relph defines it. Further, in the ways in which Marfa has become a tourist attraction through its various cultural productions, it's just another place of tourism, where the locals experience their insider Marfa and the tourists experience a very specific, produced outsider Marfa. Marfa can be divided into two identities: the place of the locals and the place of the tourists. But as the details of place are uncovered and the stories of the residents are heard, Marfa's placelessness disappears for me. Instead, this small and remote town, similar to many other small and remote towns elsewhere, becomes a unique place, defined by where its history meets its tourism meets its geography.

What does it mean to be placeless when looking at Marfa on a superficial level? What does it mean to live in a tiny town where the nearest commercial airport is three hours away by car? Is this a placeless place for those who don't see it as anything special? Does this contrarily give Marfa that much more richness and meaning to someone who makes the journey to get here? Marfa is special to those who choose to see it as something special. Those who neither know of nor care to learn about Donald Judd and his works, but who intimately know Marfa, have an entirely different experience of place. It can be special to them for entirely different reasons.

Marfa is also a site of pilgrimage for some. A pilgrimage is defined as "some form of deliberate travel to a far place intimately associated with the deepest, most cherished axiomatic values of the traveler."[14] Traditionally, pilgrimage refers to a spiritual quest, but secular pilgrimages can follow the same structure as traditional religious ones. A religious pilgrimage is sacred only because its followers have previously defined the destination or journey as sacred. Hence, any journey can be defined as a pilgrimage, depending on how the traveler views the destination. To some travelers to Marfa, the place has a sacred element, whether it's the sacredness of the art found at the Chinati Foundation or the sacredness of the landscape.

The focus of a pilgrimage may often be on the journey itself and not necessarily the destination. The longer and perhaps harder the journey, the more rewarding the trip becomes. The art critic Michael Kimmelman writes that "remoteness and exclusivity are attractions to those who appreciate the privileged view."[15] I think about this in terms of Marfa. It is certainly remote to most—is that a part of what makes it attractive? Do the remoteness and the journey necessary make it inherently exclusive? I suppose that depends on what you are looking to find when you get here, and whether or not you find it.

A shrine to the Virgin Mary stands in the yard of a small dilapidated home at the former entrance to Fort D. A. Russell. The late Hector Sanchez saw an apparition of the Virgin Mary in 1994 in his backyard and felt compelled to build the shrine in response.[16] This is a place of reverence to Catholic pilgrims, much like the Chinati Foundation is for art pilgrims, but what is most interesting is that these two sets of pilgrims likely have no knowledge of the others' intentions and purpose. The place of Marfa, for each, is an entirely separate experience, and although their paths may literally cross, they are otherwise oblivious to each other. The art patrons are on a pilgrimage to Chinati, while the religious patrons are on a pilgrimage to the shrine to the Virgin Mary. Chinati's acreage is fenced and protected, and the interior spaces are clean and minimal, but the yard in which this shrine is located is scattered with debris, some of which are the leftover gifts from the pilgrims and others just the physical markings of a family's backyard. For those who have traveled to Marfa to see this shrine, place means something very different.

If uniformity across elements of modern life is dull or sterile, then what is uniform in Marfa? There is the standard Dairy Queen, there are two Stripes, one of which has a Subway, and there is the Dollar General. These branded stores are found throughout the country and frequently act as an anchor to a small town. The Dairy Queen is the same in Marfa as it is in next-door Alpine, and were you to go to a Dairy Queen in any other state, you would see identical offerings on the menu. Sameness offers consistency. These uniform, sterile components of Marfa—or anywhere—actually tell quite a revealing story. Even if these places of uniformity are non-places, they are also where much of the detail occurs.

If Larry McMurtry can wax poetic about the happenings of the Dairy Queen in Archer City, Texas,[17] then I want to go to the Dairy

The shrine to the Virgin Mary, 2012.

Queen in Marfa to engage with real people of Marfa. What is this real Marfa? It is the Marfan who is making an average salary of $42,000.[18] It is the Marfan who works on a ranch or runs a garage. Yes, the Chinati intern or the German tourist or the owner of the coffee shop may stop in there from time to time, but the Dairy Queen has no pretense or expectation. It has cheap and simple fried food. While not all locals may engage with the various art offerings, almost all locals and tourists at one point or another will engage with the DQ. At the Dollar General, I can find an assortment of discounted household items just as I can in any other Dollar General in the country. I can also interact with locals and tourists alike, again without any pretense or expectation. If there is any expectation, it is that I will fill my basket with a few needed items and be done with it. Is this a comforting thought or simply another component of life to live and quickly be forgotten?

While I argue that Marfa is a special place, for many reasons but ultimately owing to the impact of Donald Judd, it remains for some just another small town in America. Even the grid of the town shows just how similar it is to other towns. There is the central courthouse, the four quadrants that expand from this center, the railroad that divides the town again into north and south. There are unique restaurants in Marfa: Stellina and the Capri; there is a small independent bookstore: Marfa Book Company; there are scattered shops showcasing local and Mexican crafts: Mirth, Freda. Big towns, wherever in the world they may be, are themselves summaries of the world, with ethnic, cultural, religious, social, and economic diversity, but I don't have to limit this notion to the large town or city. The idea of a worldly, cultural summation can also be found in small towns. While Marfa may have the only Buns N' Roses, or Frama coffee shop, or Mando's Restaurant, these establishments (the greasy spoon, the coffee shop, the cheap Mexican restaurant) represent which elements collectively make and create any town, anywhere.

Of course the journey, the experience of getting from Austin to Marfa, is exactly what the idea of placelessness is dismissing. The journey can be the reward. The journey is a key component, and could even be more interesting than any restaurant or gallery that one visits while in Marfa, depending on where one's interest lies. Some folks ultimately miss a lot of the charm and beauty of Marfa because they are too caught up with "seeing" everything—and once something is "seen," it can be checked off a list and forgotten. Once a photograph has been taken, documenting a person or an event in a space at a time, it's back in the car and on to the next location, the next photograph.

"A place without a story is really nowhere at all."[19] In this way Marfa is a collection of stories as varied and diverse as its residents and visitors. Some of the placing of Marfa is focused on a very specific agenda—that of fine art and culture—but Marfa's place is not so easily distilled. Each character in the many stories of Marfa is using the space to meet her own demands and intentions. The shared spaces of Marfa are produced and maintained, and there is a constant recycling of space, because small towns have to change, too. The surrounding mountains and desert terrain protect Marfa, but more than this, its physical geography protects it. The distance to the highways and major airports and cities protects it. The lack of water and resources protects it. The hidden, nonheadlined daily workings of its residents protect it. There is more to life than landscape, but "to divorce life from landscape is to invite the kind of alienation all too apparent in the world."[20] Marfa's identity remains tied to and dependent on its physical landscape but also its cultural and social landscape.

The first time I traveled to Marfa, in 2007, I befriended a pilot, Burt, who runs a business out of the small airport north of town, the Marfa Municipal Airport. Burt has lived in Marfa for over a decade and is invested in Marfa in a very specific way as a pilot. One day we took off in his small Cessna and headed south to the airfield so that I could photograph from above the closed and decaying military installation. We cruised at 1,000 feet, and then started spiraling down, lowering our altitude with each complete turn so that I could get different perspectives. As we leveled out at our lowest elevation, Burt acted as if we were going to land on one of the runways, a mimicked touch-and-go, but instead flew about 6 feet above the ground so that I could take a closer look at the installation.

One can see clear imprints on the landscape of the army airfield when looking from above via the satellite photos on Google Maps. Trying to see a closed airfield from the ground is deceptive because you can't experience the complete layout. To the pedestrian, the concrete or asphalt is broken; each crack is an opportunity for green foliage. The runways grow more vegetation than the flight line because of the difference in asphalt grade and are therefore distinguished by large trees, whereas the flight line is less verdant. The concrete foundations from former buildings dot the landscape but make no sort of larger impression on the space. All this you may notice when you are physically standing on the airfield. The space occupies the ground in a horizontal framework that is invisible to the passing motorist. Many airfields go unnoticed because they have no vertical identity.

To get 2,000 or 3,000 feet above an airfield, however, is to see a new space emerge, and when one is flying commercially at even higher elevations, airports are among the most noticeable landmarks. The imprint is unmistakable, and the runways, flight lines, and foundations come together as one complete whole, whereas on the ground they appear jumbled. It is at this higher elevation that the airfield is no longer an abandoned or closed, forgotten landscape. From the ground, the airfield is humble, a secret landscape. From above, its history is pronounced, demanding attention. Nature is an active player working against the airfield, but the airfield has perseverance. It wants to stay, to be remembered.

Much like the experience of its abandoned airfield from above, the experience of art via Marfa and the work of Donald Judd requires changing your perspective. You have to see the work at different times of day, move around the work, so that you can witness the change in color and light that allows the work to pulsate. This experience is how space becomes place, and it is a process that takes time and patience. The more time I spend in Marfa as a tourist, the more the place reveals itself to me. I say this repeatedly because I don't think it is an obvious notion. Tourists do not spend weeks or months in Marfa, or anywhere. They spend a weekend, or perhaps a week, and that is frankly not enough time to really get to know a place. In many ways, you have to remove the superficial draws of tourism from your agenda, as they can prevent you from seeing a place in its entirety.

By the time I got into a glider with Burt, he had already taken me up on two aerial shoots on previous visits. He is a friendly and knowledgeable pilot. He directed me into the seat of the small, white, and very lightweight glider, or sailplane, and within a few minutes the tow plane started to move. A young boy, who was in town from Dallas with his family specifically to go flying, held the glider's wing balanced from the ground before the plane gathered speed and then took off. Flying in a glider with the tow line feels almost as if an umbilical cord is keeping you alive (which in a way is exactly what it is), and the tension on the line exerts a subtle physical reminder of the connection between the two flying machines. Within a few minutes, Burt and I were at a high enough elevation that the tow plane could release us.

Right at that moment, when the umbilical cord comes off, you are weightless. And then that moment doesn't stop. The tow plane started to descend, but Burt and I continued in an ever-so-slight spiral that, if done properly, can last for hours.

The military's choosing of Marfa for the World War II airfield was largely based on the preexistence of Fort D. A. Russell. Still, the weather conditions made for yearlong training, and this has translated into yearlong gliding for Burt. Marfa is situated between the Pacific Ocean to the west, which brings dry air, and the Gulf of Mexico to the east, which brings moist air, and what results is a dew point line—also called the Marfa front—that creates a lifting point in the air. Pockets of warm air are what keep a glider in the sky, so to stay in the air as long as possible, a pilot needs to either stay in that warm pocket or move in and out of multiple ones. Gliding is both a science and an art, as evidenced by the technology and skill required and the beauty in how a glider smoothly rolls through the sky. Even the aircraft is a work of art, and Burt makes a parallel from the minimalism of a glider to the minimalism of much of the art in Marfa. I take the connection further back to Le Corbusier:[21] the aircraft design utilizes exactly what it needs and nothing more. A longtime reporter in Marfa has said there is "everything you need and nothing more in Marfa. There is no excess at all."[22] Seeing Marfa from above allows me to visualize this sentiment in the form of the town's small grid and quaint footprint.

Marfa is a landscape, a space, and a place. It is, for some, placeless because it is just another small town, but looking at the details of its physical and cultural structure, it becomes rich with character and detail that both define the town and set it apart from other locations. Marfa's physical geography and location have contributed to the ways in which its cultural identity has been shaped, and they continue to do so. Like all landscapes, Marfa is constructed and means different things to different people, depending on how the space is used and for what purpose. At any given time, Marfa is host to both residents and tourists, and Marfa's regular population is composed of various types of residents. These folks experience Marfa differently, and the smallness of the town and the lack of excess underlie a sometimes-hidden and complicated structure. Through experience of Marfa as a place, this structure can reveal itself, and it is through this process that the detail, beauty, and strangeness of Marfa are made tangible.

CHAPTER 4

DONALD JUDD IN MARFA

☐

"Judd is the great-grandfather of beautiful isolation," says my friend in Marfa.

I think of the people I have come to know in Marfa and how each of them might respond to that statement. I suppose if they are fans of Judd—if they like his work—they might agree. But to someone who is native to Marfa, who maybe doesn't care enough to have an opinion about it, they might think this place was beautifully isolated enough without Judd. Still, there is a particular aesthetic in Marfa rooted in Judd's vision, and this aesthetic has been given value because of Marfa's popularity and growth as a place of tourism. But it didn't just happen overnight. The Marfa aesthetic, and its exposure to the rest of the world, has a patriarch—a great-grandfather, if you will—in the artist Donald Judd.

The placing of Marfa in contemporary culture can be explicitly traced to the arrival of this incoming artist in the early 1970s. Between the years 1971 and 1994, Judd explored his ideas on art, life, and space, using the town as his canvas. After Judd's sudden and unfortunate death in 1994, an incoming wave of residents further helped expand Marfa in the form of new businesses and foundations. These new spaces allowed for a slow but continuous growth in Marfa, which has contributed to its current identity as a place of tourism. Without the presence of Judd, what would have become of Marfa is left to speculation, but many natives agree that Marfa had been "dying on the vine" with "no traffic, no nothing"[1] before his arrival, with countless businesses shuttered and streets empty. That Marfa's beauty and isolation would have perhaps drawn some other artist or artists is entirely possible, but I'm not sure there's any point in entertaining the "what-ifs." Marfa's establishment as a center of art and tourism ultimately rests with Donald Judd's work here.

Yet, today Marfa is no longer only about Donald Judd. It has become a place of inspiration for many creatives, as demonstrated by the various types of cultural productions available. This evolution of Marfa further places it on the cultural map but also adds some superficiality, perhaps, to its identity. By way of written and visual journalism, in addition to social media's presence and influence, Marfa's quirkiness and strangeness are made even more a spectacle, which in turn contributes to a particular expectation on the part of the tourist. Marfa's popularity has in some ways narrowed its identity to the outside, which presents the tourist with a greater challenge upon his or her arrival to town. On the surface, Marfa may seem like a simple small town, and in a lot of ways it is just that. However, its history, environment, climate, location, and economy—not to mention the arts—all contribute to its rich and complex identity.

Donald Judd was born in 1928 in Excelsior Springs, Missouri, and died in 1994 in Manhattan at the age of sixty-five. He served in the army from 1946 to 1947 as an engineer for the Corps of Engineers, traveling to Korea. Afterward he studied philosophy at Columbia University and did work toward a master's degree in art history that he never completed. He also studied art at the Art Students League in New York. Until his mostly permanent move to Marfa in the 1970s, he lived and worked in New York City, at first supporting himself by writing art criticism. His writing places him in a specific context in the art world, and in many ways it was strategic: he became the proverbial voice of a generation of young artists. Through his hundreds of reviews, succinct and deliberate in their delivery (on Morris Louis: "This show is much better than Louis' previous one, although it is mixed in quality"),[2] Judd developed his own ideas on art and space, which in large part prepared the reader for Judd's way of thinking. The art show reviews, the magazine pieces summarizing his theories and ideas, and his later writing on Marfa that allowed him to articulate his thoughts on art and architecture amass to a sizable body of work that gives access to the mind of an opinionated, complex, and talented artist.

In Judd's best-known essay, "Specific Objects,"[3] published in 1965, he explores the varied qualities of what he believes to be the best new work being created, which is "neither painting nor sculpture" but "related, closely or distantly, to one or the other." Painting, he writes, is "a rectangular plane placed flat against the wall," and it is this structure that inherently limits the outcome. The rectangular plane "determines and limits" the space in and around the painting. Sculpture is "made part by part, by addition, composed." The "usual materials" of wood and metal limit the result. The contemporary work being produced at the time of his writing was moving past the historic qualities of painting and sculpture. From the removal of the artist's hand ("Art could be mass-produced"), to the varied industrial materials in use, to products that are "simply forms," these contemporary objects "are specific."

Despite the fact that he is talking about the work of his peers throughout the essay, Judd's writing is really a way to justify his own work and perhaps guarantee its placement in art history.[4] He wrote that "it isn't necessary for a work to have a lot of things to look at . . . The thing as a whole, its quality as a whole, is what is interesting."[5] I think this is a good summary of his work in general, but sometimes I wonder how clear this is. There are definitely not "a lot of things" to look at with Judd's work; it's intentionally simple. The quality as a whole, though, is harder to decipher, and to quote the *New York Times* art critic Roberta Smith, "There is a kind of narrative experience."[6] I think Judd's best work changes as you walk around it (much like my airfield wall), so the quality as a whole is a fluid thing, or a narrative. But the larger works at Chinati can't really be taken in as a whole—in particular, the one hundred aluminum pieces are divided into two buildings, and the outdoor concrete pieces are too big to get a sense of their whole at once.

Written at a time when Clement Greenberg and Michael Fried were the leading art journalists, Judd's writing is in general disagreement with their respective voices.[7] In his "Complaints, Part I,"[8] Judd briefly articulates why he thinks both Greenberg and Fried are wrong in their criticism. Greenberg writes "only approval and disapproval" while not adding anything to the thinking of an artist's work, Judd says, and he writes that Fried's *Art and Objecthood*, originally published in 1967, is "stupid." Judd's succinct, straightforward approach to criticizing both art and the art critics gives his generation a specific voice as well. Just as Judd is challenging the methods of his fellow artists, he is not afraid to challenge art's placement in history as defined by the best-known critics of the time. He even says as much, in an essay from 1984: "The art magazines are not a reflection of what is happening and never have been. Unfortunately they are accepted later as reliable history. It should be remembered that they are not."[9]

In 1968, Judd bought 101 Spring Street in Manhattan's Soho neighborhood, and his modifications and installations there define—for Judd—both living and work spaces. Their sparse design is touted as working with the building's preexisting architecture and history, something Judd was interested in. It's a beautiful space to walk through, if only for the serenity and contrast afforded to the visitor as compared to the bustling activity of the city outside. The Judd Foundation only opened 101 Spring for visitors in 2013, after a lengthy restoration, and it offers about a dozen tours throughout the week. Tour groups are small, and advanced booking is necessary; the whole experience through the space's five floors lasts about ninety minutes.

Having spent much time in Marfa by the time I made it to 101 Spring Street, I was expecting a sort of mini-Marfa within the building, and a mini-Marfa is what I got. There certainly are many similarities between the five floors in Soho and the many spaces in Marfa: there is Judd-designed furniture and some of his own art, of course, along with the art of his peers and friends. The small corner library in the Soho space balloons into a massive one in Marfa; his farmhouse table in Soho multiplies into many at the Arena in Marfa; even the largest work of art—a Flavin in the bedroom—has its sister piece in Marfa, taking up six bunkers at Chinati. Judd had taken his aesthetic from New York and injected it into a small Texas town, expanding his ideas because he had so much space with which to play.

The bed on the top floor—essentially what amounts to slats of wood placed directly on the floor, with two mattresses on top—is jarring in its simplicity and utility. In the closet hang Judd's clothes, just as he had left them, and a massive brown fur jacket—rabbit maybe?—catches my eye. It looks just like one that my stepmother wears in the winter.

"Was this Julie's?" I ask the guide, referring to Judd's ex-wife, Julie Finch.

"No, that was Judd's."

I picture Judd shuffling around Soho in jeans, boots, long hair, and a large, flamboyant fur coat.

"That is awesome," I say. The guide agrees.

Judd's Marfa project is considered the second, much larger iteration of his ideas on art and life, on art and architecture, and on architecture and history.[10] Judd was able to weave his interests and the history of the spaces he overtook into one continuous, complex, fluid identity. For Judd, art was to be lived with, was a part of the interior design of a space, and it should be permanent. "The main reason for this is to be able to live with the work and think about it, and also to see the work placed as it should be."[11] Further, his work was not simply a painting on a flat surface, mounted on a wall. Nor was it a sculpture of expected material, displayed on an expected podium. Judd's work was a part of the room, and its structure seemed to be an extension of the floor or wall, as if it had been built there along with the surrounding architecture.

Judd became increasingly skeptical of museums after seeing his work damaged by being moved and installed in spaces that were ill suited to the art,[12] and he wrote a great deal about the problems, as he saw them, of museums. Museums were crowded and did not allow for an ideal interaction between the work and its viewer, which Judd thought should take plenty of time and space.[13] For Judd, the consideration of a work's installation was equally weighted with the work itself.[14] Further, the installations in museums often took the form of an anthology, a linear progression of work by date, which is one way to present art but not the only one. Judd did not see art as being so neat and tidy, and he didn't think that one piece from one artist could accurately reflect that artist's vision. Instead, Judd wanted to permanently install a large quantity of work from one artist, thus providing an entirely different relationship between the viewer and the work. This way of installing would provide an intense, saturated collection where the viewer could visually get lost in the richness and quantity of art by this one artist, and in the space itself. Judd's decision to disassociate himself, physically, from the art world would eventually lead him to Marfa.

In 1946, Judd had written a telegram to his mother from Van Horn, Texas, about 90 miles northwest of Marfa, where he had briefly passed through with the army.[15] He would say later that he remembered the landscape of West Texas and was fond of it. In 1963, Judd traveled to Tucson to visit his sister and wrote of his time, "I loved the land around Tucson chiefly because you could see it."[16] In 1968, he traveled from Colorado to Arizona, Utah, and New Mexico with his wife and two children, and the following year drove throughout Baja California, looking for an open landscape without a lot of people. He wanted land that was "undamaged,"[17] a seemingly impossible feat in the modern day. In 1971, he traveled through the Big Bend, including Marfa, where he rented a house the following summer. In 1973, he began to purchase property in Marfa, the first being two former airplane hangars from the old Marfa airport,[18] which had previously been moved into downtown in the 1930s. The next year he purchased the rest of that property, now known as "the Block," and built a high wall around the entire space using old adobe blocks from structures that had been torn down.[19] In 1975, Judd became a resident of Texas and began to spend a significant amount of his time in Marfa.

View of the Block and its surrounding adobe wall, 2011.

The harsh nature of the Texas sun has imposed on many downtown Marfa buildings the use of dark and opaque glass, or the use of thick butcher paper over interior windows, to block its rays. Judd began using this tactic when he started purchasing property, and although it was a practical solution to Marfa's heat, it nevertheless confounded some residents, who weren't used to downtown spaces being shut off to them in this way. To the local who has no vested interest in Judd or his art, the tall adobe walls that form the Block and the dark windows of his other downtown buildings can message "Go away." On my first trip to Marfa, as I walked down the street the place as a whole felt very empty. It was only when opening a door and venturing inside that I realized another world was happening on the inside of everything. It is understandable that some locals would not have taken to Judd or understood his intentions. These high walls and opaque windows create an additional sense of emptiness that constructs an interior and an exterior world, or private and public space. I wonder if Judd considered how his actions would be interpreted by the community. I spoke with one Marfa native who said she didn't know what he was doing but felt that he must have had something to hide. She referred to Judd's spaces cryptically as "the stores." In a letter to the editor from a 1999 *Big Bend Sentinel*,[20] a former Marfa resident articulated her distaste for the physical condition of Marfa's public spaces:

> Main street is no longer the focal point of the town, and the beautiful historic courthouse seems to be taken for granted. But the most disturbing phenomenon to see is all the adobe walls built within the town. The abundance of houses and buildings encased by these walls gives the appearance of secrecy, the appearance of deception, and most of all the appearance of ostracization of an entire town. It is as if the entities involved are saying, "Embrace me but do not come in!"

Hers is a valid concern, and it represents a clashing of cultures that began with Judd's arrival in Marfa and his subsequent accumulation of property, and then was continued by the incoming residents after his death. Judd was both an outsider and an insider to Marfa, and his transformation of space in Marfa perhaps contributed to the natives' skepticism of his foreign artistic practice. He also, I'm told, "stomped around town with his boots and denim shorts." I imagine him as part recluse and part antiestablishment, but also in need of validation. He did, after all, want to build something in Marfa that would attract visitors.

Between 1978 and 1979, Judd began a partnership with the Dia Art Foundation that would allow him to purchase more land, with the understanding that he was developing an alternative museum in conjunction with Dia. The Dia Art Foundation, established in 1974 by Heiner Friedrich and Philippa de Menil, has supported a number of what some would call alternative, often land-based and site-specific, art installations in permanent spaces in numerous locations in the United States and abroad.[21] The projects the foundation is interested in are those that "cannot obtain sponsorship or support from traditional commercial and private sources because of their nature or scale."[22] Dia supported the creation of Walter De Maria's *The Lightning Field* in New Mexico, from 1977, and De Maria's *The Vertical Earth Kilometer* in Kassel, Germany, from the same year. In 1999, Dia acquired Robert Smithson's *The Spiral Jetty* (1970), located in Utah's Great Salt Lake. It has also extended its reach to produce web-based art projects and public programming, not to mention its excellent museum spaces, Dia: Beacon and Dia: Chelsea, in addition to various sites around Manhattan.

It's worth looking further into the history of Dia, because it connects Marfa to Houston. Marfa may be the darling of the art world—and in this way closely connected to New York in particular—but it is very much a Texas place. Philippa de Menil (who adopted the name Fariha Friedrich after embracing Sufi Islam and marrying Friedrich in 1979)[23] was the fifth child born to Dominique and John de Menil, Houston art patrons and perhaps most famously known for building the Menil Foundation and the Rothko Chapel, both in Houston. Dominique was the middle of three daughters of Conrad Schlumberger, of the Schlumberger oil fortune (Schlumberger was established in 1934 by both Conrad and his brother, Marcel), and she married Jean de Menil (who later became John in the United States) in 1931. In 1938, John began working for Schlumberger, and it is this position that brought them to Houston, where the American headquarters were located. They were introduced to the arts, in New York, by the French Dominican priest Father Marie-Alain Couturier and would eventually amass one of the world's largest private art collections. The story of Schlumberger, his children, and their children is a fascinating one, worthy of its own book. The five children of Dominique and John all became art collectors in their own right, and the clan as a whole has contributed greatly to the arts through various philanthropic ventures, including Dia.[24]

This early iteration of what is now called the Chinati Foundation was first called the Marfa Project, and later the Art Museum of the Pecos. Through their partnership, Judd and Dia were able to purchase the former Fort D. A. Russell, which was in poor condition, having suffered years of neglect. Together they purchased some forty buildings and 340 acres of land,[25] and in total Dia invested over $5 million dollars in the Marfa Project between 1979 and 1984.[26] However, Judd and Friedrich began to disagree on the path that the museum would take, and Judd wanted more control over the decisions affecting the project.[27] There also was the matter of finances. The price of oil dropped in the 1980s, which meant that Schlumberger stock dropped, and Judd's patron no longer could support his vision. Philippa and Friedrich's spending had gotten out of control, and Dominique had to step in to regain control and put an end to the hemorrhaging of money that was occurring. As the result of a legal battle between the artist and the foundation,[28] Judd was able to break his partnership with Dia and keep all of the spaces in Marfa, as well as the art that had been purchased or had its manufacturing paid for, under a new nonprofit status and name. In 1986, the Chinati Foundation (often referred to as just "Chinati") was born, named for the nearby mountain range. Until Judd's death in 1994, he provided all the funding for Chinati, which allowed him complete control over its development. Considering the link from Chinati to Dia, and in turn to Houston and oil money, it is in this way that Marfa has always been a close associate to the rest of Texas.

Judd's work in Marfa was slow and studied, and his original plan of housing permanent installations of his work and that of his two friends John Chamberlain and Dan Flavin would grow to include in its permanent collection the work of twelve artists. Some of this work was made for placement in Marfa by way of the early in-residence program (essentially Judd inviting his friends and peers to visit and create something), and some of it was purchased or traded for by Judd and then permanently installed. Judd's development of space in Marfa was an organic process, building on each purchase and renovation of property and on the work of the artists who visited. Judd had a vision, but he did not have a particular timeline of how and when work would be made and installed. In retrospect, Judd's vision of Chinati seems as if it were meticulously laid out from the beginning,[29] but Judd's Marfa project was an ongoing process, curated and organized along the way. The success of the Chinati Foundation was in large part due to the work done after Judd's death, when its three staff members[30] were forced to find funding, build an endowment, and find the institution's footing without the largess of its creator. One can only speculate on Chinati's path had its creator not died, and Judd certainly attained an iconic status after his death.

In 1994, Judd died of lymphoma in New York. The Chinati Foundation oversees the contemporary museum in Marfa, and the Judd Foundation, created in 1996, is in charge of his living and work space in both Marfa and its environs and in New York at 101 Spring Street.[31] These two foundations are separate entities and can generally be referred to as Judd's public (Chinati) and private (Judd) spaces. Marfa's current identity stretches beyond this reach, and in many ways Judd is now a backdrop to Marfa, like an old cathedral.

Judd's spaces of Marfa go beyond any structured notion of art, place, and architecture. Even with his simple furniture designs[32] he has brought art into the everyday. To see the vision of Donald Judd is not to see one object, or a collection of objects in a room. Although a specific focus of Marfa's identity—there are still countless natives who have never toured the Chinati or Judd Foundations or any of the other gallery spaces and have no interest in doing so—Judd's spaces of Marfa have placed Marfa in a very specific, arts-focused frame of mind. That the attention given to Marfa is often focused on this arts identity is not an insult to the locals;[33] instead it is a product of the town's recent history. Marfa's popularity is so heavily focused on the arts that this is often what drives writers and journalists to visit. If anything, the locals can take comfort in knowing that *their* Marfa is much more complex than any article could make it out to be. In this way, their Marfa remains somewhat protected.

If you are used to traditional museums, touring the Chinati Foundation is a different kind of experience. Chinati is a museum that incorporates the landscape of West Texas and uses the physical structures of its history, including Fort D. A. Russell. Perhaps what is most obvious needs repeating: it requires a journey, an intention, and commitment on the part of the visitor. This journey to Marfa is inconvenient, but this is what defines a pilgrimage.[34] Through the journey to get here, the space of Marfa becomes place—an intimate, personal experience.

When one is a visitor to Marfa, and to Judd's spaces in particular, there is a collective sense that sights must be seen, that even a personalized journey made by one is never an entirely solo journey. It is a journey made by many, and to make it is to partake in a shared experience that unifies the varied travelers. Despite the fact that each tourist has his or her own specific experience, these experiences collectively create the site. The Chinati Foundation is the space, but through the pilgrimage of the tourist, it becomes place. The small guided tours—the only way to see the space outside of the annual Open House weekend in October, when you can wander through the spaces unguided and at your own pace—take up most of your day and can be a physically exhausting experience. There are no museum benches on which to rest, and you go in and out of the heat with frequency, and walk a great deal.

The full tour of Chinati starts at 10:00 a.m. or 10:30 a.m. and ends at 4:30 p.m. or 5:00 p.m., and takes you through every component of the museum in addition to the rotating temporary show installed at the time of your visit.[35] There's a two-hour lunch break, which is a good time to take a nap, eat, and hydrate. That's four total hours of walking and seeing, where seeing is an active function that takes energy of the mind and body. There is, in essence, a lot to take in. Besides Donald Judd's pieces, Chinati's full collection includes work by Dan Flavin, John Chamberlain, Richard Long, Carl Andre, Ingólfur Arnarsson, Roni Horn, Ilya Kabakov, David Rabinowitch, John Wesley, Claes Oldenburg and Coosje van Bruggen, and Robert Irwin. Collectively, Donald Judd curated most of the works represented, and each work is given its own dedicated space.

The selections tour is only two and a half hours long and takes you through the installations of the four central artists of Chinati: Donald Judd, John Chamberlain, Dan Flavin, and Robert Irwin. (Of note is that Irwin is the most recent addition, completed in 2016.) Either tour is an interesting way to experience art: it is specific, guided, and structured, and the scheduling takes you through each building at nearly the same time each day. I believe this is important, for most of Judd's work—really, the crux of his aesthetic and design—is that his art is activated by the viewer and by the light's shifting influence on the objects, depending on the sun's position in the sky. Because of the museum's structure, there is a very specific, limited amount of time, at a particular time of day, in which to experience the art. This creates a hypercontrolled environment that gives the viewer a specific landscape of place in which to view the art. Judd created an alternative museum designed for the art, to make the experience of art more open, but in actuality it's probably more structured than any other modern museum space.

Chinati is aware of this and has made efforts in recent years to make the space more open to visitors. I spoke with Jenny Moore, Chinati's director since 2013, about this particular dilemma. The problem of staffing and funding is unfortunately a blocker, but it is her goal to continue to expand visitor access and make a visit "less restrictive."[36]

My favorite work in Chinati is the work that is most successful in terms of working with and for the landscape, as well as the site's history: Judd's *15 untitled works in concrete*, fabricated by the CRS company in Midland-Odessa over a period of roughly four years (1980–1984).[37] The first thing you notice about these fifteen concrete boxes sitting in a low field on the east side of the Chinati Foundation is that they are bare and plain. As you make your way down one of the narrow footpaths, you also begin to realize that they are massive. The best time to view them, in my opinion, is in the late afternoon, because during the summer midday hours, the heat and sun can be stifling. (During the winter months, this is less of a problem, although then you have the desert cold to contend with.) Additionally, depending on when you view them, the boxes' contrast and shadows change, both of which are a central component to experiencing them. Chinati's front gate opens at 9:00 a.m. and closes at 5:00 p.m., and within this time period a visitor is welcome to walk down to these concrete works at no charge. I like to walk around them shortly before closing time.

Let me be clear about *15 untitled*, because it is not easily loved: the piece comprises a bunch of massive concrete boxes placed on a field. The works are installed on a roughly north-south line on what was once the fort's polo ground, and as such it is a relatively flat surface that sits lower than the rest of Chinati. Each cluster contains anywhere from two to six concrete boxes, and each cluster is arranged differently, some forming more linear configurations with ninety-degree angles and others forming circular configurations. As is standard with Judd's work, the outer dimensions are consistent, but the detail on each piece is varied. Some boxes have open sides at the long end; others have open sides at the short end. Each box is open on at least one side but no more than two. The boxes themselves are 5 meters long and 2.5 meters deep.[38] Each box is symmetrical in its outer use of space, but the difference in each box and in their unique configurations creates a specific place. The simplicity of each form reveals individual aspects as you investigate each piece and each configuration.

As I walk around and in the boxes, I realize how hard it is to fully "see" each piece when too close, a reminder that perspective is just as important as location. At the same time, walking around and in the boxes opens up the surrounding landscape. The swooshing of cars along Route 67 to the east of the concrete structures places me in an active Marfa, but otherwise the sounds around me are those of nature: the singing of a cricket, the scurry of a lizard, the buzzing of a bee, and the gentle breeze against the vegetation. When I step inside a box and move toward its interior, the space becomes a little quieter, unless there is an unseen insect inside whose sounds create

View of *15 untitled works in concrete*, 1980–1984, 2012. Donald Judd Art
© 2017 Judd Foundation/Artists Rights Society (ARS), New York.

a small echo. The temperature inside the box is noticeably cooler, and gives another sensual focus to the experience of the work: the inside and the outside are different spaces.

The concrete is uniform but rough, and there are imperfections in each form due to time and the environment: a tiny gap at one crease, a larger gap at another. These imperfections are perhaps telling: despite Judd's obsession with precision, his work has become decidedly imprecise. Some of the creases allow sunlight into the interior space, giving another contrast between light and dark, inside and outside. The shadows created by the sun have allowed a very specific type of vegetation around each box: the areas of shade provide for richer growth, while the areas that remain outside of any shade are dryer, cracked, harsh. Have you lived somewhere when a tall building goes up where there was none before? Everything in its vicinity changes, shadows become consuming. What is placed onto a landscape has a direct effect on its surrounding space.

Walking along this stretch of land, I place the military bunkers and the former artillery sheds in the backdrop of these concrete shapes. The similarity in form is noticeable, and I am left with a very simple architectural space, for the bunkers themselves are cookie-cutter and simple. They represent a structured, formal design and identity that characterize the military, which now serve to characterize the Chinati Foundation. These buildings are architecture at its core: form mixed with function.

That Judd's work in concrete is visually aligned with the military architecture of the Chinati Foundation presents an obvious correlation to me. The bunkers are noticeably lacking in any sort of superfluous design or geometry. They are simple forms that historically served a specific task, and their present task is also simple. Whether housing soldiers or sculpture, there is a utility of form and purpose in the structures. They are unsophisticated but perfect in their simplicity. The architecture of military design lacks gesture, as does Judd's work. In this way his concrete boxes together form a monument to the military history of Marfa. But these *15 untitled works in concrete* are dependent on the environment they surround, which is the environment and architecture of Fort D. A. Russell. In this way they are site-specific.

I will define site-specific art as art that is created for a specific place. Some go further to say that site-specific art is made *in response to* a specific place. Still others argue that *any* art is site-specific simply because it is situated where it is.

As a genre, site-specific art gained popularity in the late 1960s and early 1970s and had a close relationship to the environment.[39] Artists were reaching out of the gallery into a tangible landscape that could prompt a different kind of reaction from the viewer. Through this new way of experiencing work, the involvement and *journey* of the viewer were paramount. The various factors of the site are what produce the work. Richard Serra's *Tilted Arc* of 1981 is an oft-repeated example of a site-specific work, famously dismantled in 1989 after a long battle with the City of New York. From Serra's perspective, it was not possible to move the piece to a different site, as had been proposed by the city. "To remove the work is to destroy the work,"[40] he lamented. Judd's installations in Marfa are meant to remain here indefinitely, thereby creating a permanent relationship with the surrounding landscape, as well as solving the problems he saw with ordinary museums. In this way Judd's work in Marfa can be seen as one massive, site-specific installation. Marfa is the work, the work is Marfa.

But I question how site-specific they actually are. Most of the work in the collection wasn't built specifically for the space—it was installed there after being acquired by Judd. So there's a sort of post-site-specificity to the museum as a whole. Even Judd's decision to move to Marfa was in part a product of chance, perhaps, because he very well could have chosen another town. He had traveled all over the Southwest, as well as Baja, and if it hadn't been for the logistical challenge of importing/exporting work to another country, he very well may have settled outside of the United States. That he chose Marfa—in large part because of its beauty—was also a product of sensibility and business. The space worked for him, so he made it work.

The two artillery sheds house Judd's *100 untitled works in mill aluminum*, fifty-two in the first building and forty-eight in the second. Each box shares the same outer dimensions but is made unique by the makings of its interior space. You enter and depart each shed on the side, working from the northern side of the field, and Judd's replacement of the garage doors with large glass panels allows an influx of sunlight to activate the space.

The artillery sheds are the first things you see on the scheduled tour, and the two buildings make the largest visual footprint on the landscape. Judd had replaced the original flat roofs with barrel-shaped metal in an attempt to control leaking, and this transformation doubled the height of each building.[41] (It also failed to solve the leaking.) It is interesting that he felt the need to install such large roofs, for they are entirely unnecessary to the experience of the inside works (the ceilings inside are not extended), and visually make a large stamp on the landscape. You can see the sheds easily from the air and from many points outside of the immediate grounds of Chinati. In Judd's words, he "turned them into architecture,"[42] but for the vernacular enthusiast, they were already architecture without his hand. The addition of the barrel roofs also could have been a deliberate attempt to separate the space from its military history—Judd had originally asked the Dia Foundation to fund new construction for his mill aluminum boxes, but his request was refused.[43] A visitor to the spaces once remarked that having a second building with aluminum boxes was just "unnecessary" and more a marker of Judd's ego.[44]

The interior space is magical. Chinati regularly offers sunrise and sunset viewings of the sheds, and it has in recent years added a daily self-guided tour of these two buildings. Viewing these pieces at different times of day allows them to further unravel themselves into objects that allow the light and colors to constantly transform before my eyes. Although each piece is unique, to try to focus on any one is "like trying to focus on a word in a paragraph in a novel."[45] Collectively, the reflections of the aluminum create colors and intensities of light that never seem to look the same. Installed in a simple alignment, the boxes seem to grow up and out of the floor, and yet at the same time, they hover. Where one box will have an open top, the interior space absorbing the light and looking dark to my eye, another box will have a closed top that sharply

One of the artillery sheds, housing *100 untitled works in mill aluminum*, 2012. Donald Judd Art © 2017 Judd Foundation/Artists Rights Society (ARS), New York.

100 untitled works in mill aluminum, 2012. Donald Judd Art © 2017
Judd Foundation/Artists Rights Society (ARS), New York.

reflects light. The boxes' shiny and smooth surfaces contrast with the roughness of the red brick and beige concrete that forms the interior space of the buildings.

Judd's overarching rubric developed into the stripping away of excessive and unnecessary forms, leaving him with simple shapes based on geometry and math coupled with the decidedly non- or anti-art use of industrial and commercial materials. These pieces are stripped of excess and gesture. To see these works, I almost have to ignore their specific shapes and impress on myself that the work does not function without me—the viewer—and the available light. The work, then, is in the experience of place that happens when I am in the sheds and moving around the space.

Dan Flavin's contribution to the Chinati Foundation was a component of Judd's original design; however, it would take about twenty-two years from concept to completion of his *untitled (Marfa project)*. Flavin was born in 1933 in Jamaica, New York, and died in 1996 at the age of sixty-three. He studied to be a priest but left to join the air force, where he was deployed to Korea. He returned to New York in 1956, studying art and immersing himself in the scene.[46] His installation at the Chinati Foundation was initiated in the 1980s, but Dia's financial troubles presumably contributed to its delay.[47] After Judd and Flavin had a falling out, it seemed as if the project might never be completed. It was through the efforts of Marianne Stockebrand, Judd's partner and the director of Chinati for sixteen years,[48] who worked with Flavin shortly before his death, that this "last great art of the 20th century"[49] was able to reach completion.

Flavin is known for his use of fluorescent tubing, industrial and limited in colors, to create sculpture and to transform the light in a given space. His work at Chinati is the only work in the collection that is artificially lighted (of course, its own material of fluorescent tubing provides the light) and takes up six of the eleven U-shaped bunkers. Using four colors—pink, green, yellow, and blue—each installation within a bunker utilizes the U shape to either hide or highlight the tubing upon first entering. The bunkers alternate, so that in the first, third, and fifth bunkers, the four elements of tubing are installed in the middle of the bottom of the U, so that their colors and intensity are not seen until I walk down the arm of the bunker and stand at the corner. In the second, fourth, and sixth bunkers, the tubing is installed at an angle at the bottom corner of the U, so that the intensity of the vertical forms is seen as soon as I enter the space. I cannot walk through each U-shaped building, and instead have to go into each arm individually, so that to view all six bunkers I open and close twelve doors. Most of the windows are no longer functional, but are filled in and recessed (so that their utility is referenced but not accessed), but two windows at the entrance side of each arm allow a modest amount of sunlight into the room.

From the outside, the walls of the plain bunkers hide their illuminated interiors. It is in the methodical process of going into and out of each arm, into and out of the sunlight, my eyes adjusting with each entrance and departure, that the work comes together into a whole. It is a repetitive process, but it is revealing in the way that the fluorescent light interacts with the white walls and interacts with the other fluorescents to create new colors and the illusion of color. While I may be alone in one arm, the adjacent one may have people inside, so I may hear the movements and echoes of these bodies unseen. If I am entirely alone in a bunker, the steady pulse of the fluorescent electric light is the only sound available. It's eerie and wonderful and calming.

Flavin's work in Marfa places me in an artificial space for which the interior is much different than the exterior environment. It is a contrast between natural sunlight and human-made industrial light. Like Judd's boxes, Flavin's fluorescent forms lack reference and gesture. The colors are playful, and the deception their combinations offer to the eye builds on this playfulness.

John Chamberlain was born in 1927 in Rochester, Indiana, and died in 2011 at the age of eighty-four. He served in the navy and studied art at the Art Institute of Chicago and at Black Mountain College, moving to New York in 1957.[50] Although he is known for using automobile scraps to create sculpture, he also worked in foam and other materials at times, and his output of sculpture is displayed directly on the floor or mounted on walls, depending on the size and construction.

Dan Flavin, *untitled (Marfa project)*, 2011. © Stephen Flavin/
Artists Rights Society (ARS), New York.

Chamberlain's installation at Chinati is outside the grounds of Fort D. A. Russell, instead housed in the former Wool & Mohair Company building, just north of the railroad tracks and across from the post office. The interior space is divided into a front room, two middle side rooms, and a large middle and then a large back room. Chamberlain's work is characterized by the use of automobile metal, bent and shaped into massive, usually bulbous shapes that contrarily seem delicate in their lightness. In Marfa, twenty-two of these pieces are grouped together, each a totem to industry. His pieces work best in this space. In other museum settings, when often clustered around dissimilar works, Chamberlain's metal doesn't work the way it does in Marfa. I think it's because the other works in the space distract from the overall effect. The occasional passing train interrupts the space of the building with its noise, but this confluence of travel—the active train outside and the passive, deceased remnants of the automobile inside—focuses the viewer into a place of technology and travel, of speed and power. In the warehouse, this speed and power are both shuttered.

The Robert Irwin project was a long time in the making.

Judd and Irwin were friends, and there's a lovely story in Lawrence Weschler's *Seeing Is Forgetting the Name of the Thing One Sees* from 1982 about Irwin heading out for a drive from his home in Los Angeles and not stopping until he got to Texas. In the spirit of Marfa and its small-world-inducing charms, Irwin happened to encounter Judd on the side of the road. Like Judd, Irwin was interested in the experience of place that his work could induce, calling his work "conditional" or "conditioned art."[51] It isn't any wonder, perhaps, that Judd would have liked to see Irwin do a piece for Chinati.

The discussions for the Irwin project began in 1999, and the plans went through much iteration, according to Chinati's associate director Rob Weiner. The Marfa local Tim Crowley, who owned the site where the Irwin piece was installed, gifted the land to Chinati explicitly for the installation of the Irwin piece. The location of the work is the old hospital building of Fort D. A. Russell, which had been slowly decaying for decades. When I first met Rob in 2007, he showed me early plans of the piece. As a lover of Irwin's work, I was immediately hooked. Originally, Irwin was invited to use the

John Chamberlain, various works, 1972–1983, 2011. © Fairweather &
Fairweather LTD/Artists Rights Society (ARS), New York.

existing walls of the hospital building, to make slight modifications to an existing structure. It would be a perfect way to reuse an old space, adding new life to a crumbling building and an important piece to Chinati's collection. However, as architects weighed in on the feasibility of the project, it was determined that the existing walls would not support Irwin's design, and ultimately Chinati decided to tear down the building in order to build a "facsimile" of it in its place that could bear the weight. Locals were not happy.

The hospital building was a beloved landmark in Marfa, if only because it had such an interesting design—a rectangular building, nearly square in shape but with longer sides than the front and back, with an opening in the front for access to the large central courtyard. There was another smaller structure in the middle of this courtyard.

But as a space of use, it was dead. The problems of its architecture, which would eventually force Chinati to decide that demolition was the only option, were the same ones that plagued Judd throughout his time in Marfa as he was building Chinati. Military buildings went up quickly and weren't necessarily expected to last, and the greatest challenge was the lack of rebar in the concrete. (It's also what has created a huge challenge for Chinati's master plan, an ambitious, costly, and necessary project to maintain the site's structures.)[52] In short, the hospital building was crumbling, and although it was possible to build separate support for the walls from the outside, it would have made no sense to install Irwin's work in that way. For these reasons, the demolition of the hospital building and installation of the Irwin piece had a significant effect on those Marfa residents who loved the old site: they were angry and saddened.[53]

And they had every right to be, for there is a bit of hypocrisy that is not easy to dismiss. In 2014, while the Irwin controversy was happening, another historic building from Fort D. A. Russell was saved from demolition due to community outcry, led by Marianne Stockebrand, now director emerita of Chinati. The "ultramodern" home that would have taken the historic home's place was "out of context" for that neighborhood.[54] How is it that a historic home was important enough to spare and yet the hospital building was not? Few laws in Marfa regulate development and preservation, which means that Marfa mainly relies on its people to do the right thing in terms of development and preservation. Chinati funded the demolition of the hospital building, and the site was deemed a "noncontributing" structure, which means that on its own it would not be eligible for protection. This, sadly, does not take away from the fact that it *did* contribute to the historical fabric of the Fort D. A. Russell site. Jenny Moore reminded me that Marianne Stockebrand is not Chinati, and Chinati took no position regarding the demolition of the home. I reached out to Marianne for comment but did not get a response.

The Irwin piece is significant for another important reason—it will likely be his last. At eighty-eight years old, Irwin is likely to leave this as his final opus to the art world, and the only freestanding structure of his design.

It was with this context in mind that I traveled to Marfa for the opening of this installation.

The opening for the Robert Irwin piece takes place over a weekend near the end of July in 2016, and Marfa is overrun with visitors—I've never seen so many people in town. I've driven in from Austin, having left early on a Saturday morning, and when I arrive in Marfa, it's about noon. I head straight to the Irwin.

What is normally a sleepy road outside of Chinati's gate is now filled with parked cars and pedestrians on the sidewalk and in the street. I park and start walking toward the hospital building. A volunteer underneath a small tent offers water and guidance. "No photography," I am told with a smile.

As I walk closer to the building I can see the central courtyard, where there is now a large installation of basalt where there used to be a small structure. The basalt is a rusted color, and the pieces are placed vertically against each other. Surrounding this is a handful of paloverde trees. The trunks are stained green, which I later learn is an adaptation that allows them to photosynthesize through their bark. Everything is new and perfect, and the building and its immediate environment have not had time to settle in. It's the complete opposite of the former hospital building's ruins, which had for decades been lying vacant without purpose or presumption.

The old hospital building (2010) and Robert Irwin's *untitled (dawn to dusk)*, 2016.
The Irwin piece is © Robert Irwin/Artists Rights Society (ARS), New York.

I can enter the building from either side, part of the front rooms now without a roof, so that the doors are inset from the start of the structure. A thin strip of wood is visible along the top of the walls on this exterior part. Again, I later learn that this was intentional, and is supposed to mimic the absence of a roof. It had been there, it had fallen in, and now is gone.

Everything is too precious. But I think that perhaps I cannot yet allow myself to be fully immersed in the piece because of my affection for the former building. It still stings, a little, to see this new and precise building in the place of what was a beautiful ruin.

On top of that, Chinati had told Marfans that the Irwin piece would be a facsimile of the hospital, but it's not. There's basalt in the middle where there once was a part of the building. This new space is supposed to be, in part, reference to or even homage to the history of the original space. But it's not. I can identify no history when absolutely nothing of the original is left.

I'm already feeling this way—defensive and put off—before I've gone inside, so I take a deep breath and smile as the volunteer opens the door for me. (There are volunteers everywhere, wearing Chinati T-shirts.) "No photography!" I am again told.

It smells like new. The building is divided into a white and a black/gray space, and I've started on the white side. A long piece of scrim runs down the length of the corridor, dividing it in two. The floors are stained concrete, and the walls are white. The windows are at intervals on both sides, and their height is a little unsettling. The bottoms are perhaps 5 feet high, and feel unnatural. This is in reference to Dutch landscape painting, according to Rob Weiner, because in Dutch landscapes there is more space on the canvas devoted to the sky, and perhaps Irwin is making a connection to the Marfa sky. People slowly walk throughout, some making quiet talk and others silently viewing. This is perhaps the busiest that this room will ever be, and the relative bustle of activity, I think, creates a different kind of experience of the space. I want to see it when there is no one else here.

Scrim, Irwin's favorite material, is a partly translucent and thin fabric that can be used for a variety of purposes, but perhaps most notably for theatrical productions. If lit from the front, scrim will reflect light, and if lit from behind, scrim will transmit light, creating silhouettes from forms or objects. Irwin has used it for years to divide space and to shape the light within space.

I walk down the long corridor, hearing and partly seeing the ghostly shadows of the people on the other side of the scrim. All light enters from the many unnaturally high windows. Halfway down the hall is a break in the scrim that aligns with a door to the central courtyard. If I stand in the middle of this break, I can look down either side of the scrim walls, which has the effect of being in a bed and playing with lifting and lowering the sheet—I feel like I'm in my own space, enveloped by this material. It's womblike.

This white scrim wall ends at the corner of the room, and, looking to the right, I see a series of additional scrim walls, this time perpendicular to me and with doorways cut out in their middles. There are three white and three black scrim walls, and as you pass through the middle of this arm, the outer white walls change to a neutral gray. On this side of the building, the scrim is black. As I make my way through the black side, a mirror image, I think about how the piece might have felt if I had started on the black side and moved to white.

Black and white, good and bad, light and dark, one Marfa and another Marfa.

After spending some time with the black scrim, I make my way back to the white side. I'm most curious about what is happening outside the windows. On the black side, nothing stands next to the building, but on the white side there is a house. There are many, many things in the house's yard—an old and rusted pickup truck, a garage half fallen in on itself, a sign that alerts me to the presence of buried cable, windows covered in corrugated metal, stacks of corrugated metal on the ground. I can't tell if anyone lives in the house, and when I view it from the front, on my walk back to the car, the overgrowth tells me that there isn't much presence or activity happening. And yet there is chaos in the back and on the side. Two more options for the duality of the Irwin construction: chaos and order.

That afternoon, there is a lecture at the theater on the making of the Irwin piece. Rob Weiner and Jeff Jamieson, a longtime assistant to Irwin, greet a standing-room-only crowd of art aficionados and walk them through the long process of seeing the piece to fruition. It has taken nearly seventeen years to get here, but I don't know how long it will take for me to warm to the piece.

The Judd Foundation—established after Judd's death and whose mission is to "maintain and preserve Donald Judd's permanently installed living and working spaces, libraries, and archives in New York and Marfa, Texas"[55]—has a process of exploration similar to Chinati's, wherein you can take a scheduled tour of the Block lasting an hour or a longer tour of the architecture studio, the art studio, and the Cobb and Whyte houses[56] lasting an additional ninety minutes. The timing for these two tours is such that you can take them both on the same day (2:00–3:30 p.m. for the longer Studios tour, 4:30–5:30 p.m. for the Block tour).[57] Again, this is a physically exhausting process. Although the work is engaging and tour groups are kept to a small number, standing and walking in and out of the Texas heat, plus entering stuffy spaces that are often much hotter than the outside, is a trying experience to the visitor. In the winter, the opposite problems of wind and chill meet you. The landscape and environment of Marfa contribute directly to the visitor experience.

For someone traveling to Marfa with the intention of touring everything that the Chinati and Judd Foundations have to offer, a weekend or long weekend visit limits your experience of Marfa to these very specific places. In this way, the art tourist to Marfa is privy to a very narrowed experience of the town.

The Block was Judd's living and work space, designed with symmetry and privacy in mind. The tall adobe wall separates an outside world from a private, interior space, and the interior grounds combine spaces of community (dining tables), relief from climate (a "cement water accumulation pond,"[58] also known as a pool), and spaces of cultivation and environment (a winter greenhouse and garden space). Judd's house and his two studios occupy much of the square footage. Within his studios Judd places some of his earlier works, and many of the pieces are themselves rejects—test pieces that did not meet Judd's standard—but in his private space offered an opportunity for his own contemplation and review.

The other spaces of the Judd Foundation take up many downtown buildings, creating a continuing environment of inside and outside space. Judd in many ways had imposed an "architectural fury"[59] on the space of Marfa, but in so doing he established a place where art, architecture, and day-to-day living come together into one interdependent whole, where the lines between them as individual functions are less defined. Many of the rooms throughout these Judd spaces contain a bed,[60] which is both sensible and representative. The beds are sensible, because Judd owned a lot of space, and moving in and out of the space could be tiresome. A bed also provided him an opportunity to sit down and be in the space with his work for as long as he chose, in marked contrast to the average experience of the standard museum visitor. The presence of a bed in each space also represents the confluence of private, personal living space with the objects, art or otherwise, that fill them. Judd's work was lived with and lived in, and this is what creates the site-specificity of his work in Marfa.

Judd's spaces in Marfa are not without criticism from the art world. The first Lannan Foundation[61] writer-in-residence in Marfa, Peter Reading, wrote:

> The artist Donald Judd deigned to descend
> here in the 1970s, and proceeded
> (courtesy of vast funding from his patron)
> to launch himself indulgently upon
> a spoilt-child, hedonistic shopping-spree
> procuring half the town.[62]

On the concrete works, the same writer wrote:

> Across the windswept, Pronghorn-browsed brown grass
> Judd's row of concrete, seven-foot-high boxes
> stretches a mile north-south, signifies zilch.[63]

For Reading, the ego of the artist is most noticeable to him as he inspects the installations in the midst of the Marfa landscape. For others, Judd's work was something not readily understood. I encountered a Marfa native who shared with me her experience with Judd at a time when the concrete works were partially complete.[64]

When she was sixteen, she worked in her dad's repair shop in town. Donald Judd would come in for electrical help and advice, and her dad worked with Judd a number of times to advise him on how best to update the electrical systems in the buildings he had purchased while preserving the integrity of the structures. She admits that she didn't care much for Judd. Here was this weird art guy buying up buildings, and the adults were skeptical, and all this she overheard and transferred to create her own skepticism of the man.

One day, Judd was in the store, and he asked her, "Young lady, why do you sneer at me?"

She was busted.

She was also honest.

"I think your art is ugly."

Judd thought about this, then asked her father if he could borrow her for a couple of hours. She was terrified. Her father acquiesced, and Judd took her out to the old polo grounds of the former fort where *15 untitled works in concrete* was in an early iteration.

"What do you see?" he asked her.

"I see concrete boxes that are obstructing the view of the landscape."

They walked down the hill a little. Same question. Same answer.

They walked farther down and sat in one of the boxes. And watched, and waited. At some point her expression had changed, which Judd noticed.

"What do you see?" Judd asked again.

She responded that she saw amazing shadows, that these shadows were moving, that she finally understood what the concrete boxes had enabled her to see. She understood then that the boxes themselves were not the art. It was the quality of light and shadow that they inspired, that her presence there was part of the work.

She and Judd talked about how she would never again see the sun in that particular place, at that particular time.

She still doesn't care much for his art—she has never toured the complete collection—but she does understand his perspective.

The very specificity that defines Judd's objects is also what can, perhaps, isolate the viewer. This native, for example, wasn't used to seeing dull concrete boxes as art, but by spending time with the space, the works became place to her, and she understood Judd's intention. Lacking any visible sign of craft or skill—unless you want to count the industrial craft of machined objects by paid laborers—the work, when viewed as an object separated from the space it is occupying, can leave the viewer cold. It is not ironic that Marfa's failing economy and emigrating community are what presented Judd with the opportunity to purchase all this real estate,[65] but it *is* ironic that the qualities that best define his work—their simplicity in both form and composition, that they need only be interesting, that they do not follow any traditionally accepted notion of either painting or sculpture—are also what isolate them.

I don't believe that a given artwork's meaning should be readily apparent, but its theoretical accessibility can make it appealing to a wider audience. To the naked eye, the simplicity of Judd's installations in Marfa might be off-putting, depending on the viewer's expectations of what art should be. One local, Lineaus Lorette, has repeatedly called Judd's work "fascist," and refers to Chinati as "Chinazi."

"I'm the anti-Chinati person in town," he tells me one afternoon.

I'm not sold on the fascist designation—if anything, the work is elitist—so I ask him to explain it to me.

"Well it's chauvinistic. Okay, so what's the definition of fascism—the definition of fascism is the corporate state. That's Mussolini's definition. It's big business controlling the economy. And minimalism is corporate art. It's elevator art. It's big, it's meant to be noncontroversial. So that's why I called it fascist art. If it's corporate art, it is fascist art."

I don't know that I would qualify Judd's work as corporate art (and he didn't like the term "minimalism" either), but I like that Lorette has such an intense hatred of Chinati. He likes being the guy to hate them.

"I think [Chinati] art is all chauvinistic. It's not meant to communicate the love of life that the artist has. Art should elicit an emotion, and [Chinati art] is art without emotion. And you don't have any place to go to after that. Where do you go to after you have taken all the emotion out of art? The desire to create is a human characteristic, but . . . I don't know where minimalism takes you."

I think of the times I've seen the aluminum works at Chinati during sunrise, and how they are filled with emotion, to the point of being a religious experience for me. But I'm not going to sell him on it, not today.

When I've spoken with locals who are not fans of Judd's work, a specific definition of art was repeated to me, over and over: art is painting. Of course, students of art history know that art is much more than that.

The correlation between class and arts consumption has been explored[66] and is directly relevant to the community of Marfa, despite the sensitive nature of the topic. What I want to say here is this: If you have neither an interest in nor an education in contemporary art, I can appreciate that Judd's work might be hard for you to understand, let alone like. I love art, and I am an artist, and I will travel hundreds of miles specifically to go see a piece of art or a museum exhibition. I realize how strange this seems to some people. So when Marfa natives see hordes of tourists pouring into town to go look at big gray boxes on the grounds of the old fort, they've got to be thinking to themselves, "What the hell are all these people doing?"

Education and income are both "strongly related to the likelihood of high-arts exposure."[67] Because Marfa is an economically disadvantaged town for many of its full-time residents, this results in many locals' disinterest in and distaste for the "high brow" collection of the Chinati Foundation and the exhibitions held in other galleries. One local has noted that in Marfa, there is not a lot of crossover between the art community and the Hispanic one, adding that despite this, there is not much animosity between the groups. When outsiders consider the presence of discrimination in Marfa, it is a class and economic distinction among its community members that they should be looking for.

Apart from locals' opinions of Judd's work, I wonder how well it holds up in terms of its placement in art history. Judd and his peers—all of whom served in the military—were against blatant displays of military power, but their strict vocabulary is just as indicative of another power (and I haven't even gotten into the gendered-ness of this kind of art; how there is only one woman in the Chinati collection). It is a power hidden behind a lack of gesture, but perhaps made more apparent by its very materiality and construction. Most of Judd's work on display in both the Chinati and Judd Foundations is heavy and cumbersome. And the fact that someone else fabricated each piece speaks to the transactions of a capitalist society, and of Judd as an author and a thinker but not a laborer. For some, the work occupies "a special sphere, aloof from politics and commerce and above personal feeling."[68] Is the focus on the object as nonart somehow depriving it of personality? Is this what the locals find so infuriating (or boring) about it? Greenberg lamented, "Minimal Art remains too much a feat of ideation, and not enough anything else."[69] Judd's writing about art shows a philosopher and an author of ideas that became work—that became tangible—at the hand of someone else. It is hard to say which is more valid: the beautiful products of his thinking that can be experienced in Marfa, or the power that these products represent. Either way, they are worth experiencing, and seeing them in combination with Judd's private spaces helps them become quite personal.

Still, the spaces of Judd's Marfa represent a specific component to the town's identity. Further, apart from docent or intern-led tours, Judd's private spaces are today without function. They are snapshots of his life, kept intact just as they were when he passed. Whereas during his life this collection of spaces represented an active, compulsive, and obsessive order of form (and with two children on the grounds, the spaces had to have been at least a little messier), in his death they have become places of entombment. These spaces were once alive, and now they are void, and they contain an almost haunting quality of emptiness despite the objects that fill them. This is also, perhaps, the irony of space, and part of what makes me feel better about the demolition of the hospital building. If you don't use space, if it is not functioning on some active level, the space inherently loses its meaning.

I want to return to Judd's "Specific Objects" essay of 1965. In it he describes the "insufficiencies" of both painting and sculpture.[70] The limitation of painting, he says, is that the medium is a two-dimensional object on a flat, square, or rectangular plane, to be set on a wall. Although painting in his lifetime was working beyond these confines,[71] for Judd, this type of historical structure could not move beyond these limitations. The elements of painting—oil and canvas, for instance—were limited by their inherent self-referencing: oil is used by artists and artists paint on canvas. In his use of industrial materials—plexiglass, concrete, plywood, and aluminum—Judd deleted the reference to art, and to art history's larger rubric. However, he didn't delete the reference to the machine and to the industry from which his specific objects are born. Judd was the designer, the architect, the visionary. He put his ideas to paper in the form of simple sketches, and then he worked with contracted and delegated companies to see his ideas come to life. He pushed art in a new direction—one without any markings of his own personality (in that he didn't actually make the work)—by using new materials and new processes. In a search for subjectivity by way of the lack of his own hand in his work, Judd instead carved out an objective place for himself by becoming one of the voices of minimalism, even though he rejected that term.[72]

As for sculpture, Judd said that it was an object that was placed on a pedestal, and this pedestal separated the object's meaning from the viewer's relationship with it. "Most sculpture is made part by part, by addition, composed." It's placed into a space, but does not create the space itself. With his specific objects, Judd produced space. "Actual space is intrinsically more powerful and specific than paint on a flat surface."[73]

If sculpture and painting cannot exist without the inherent reference to their medium, can anything exist as a pure form in itself? If Judd's objects, made specific by their geometry and placement, are not referencing a larger history of art, to what are they referring? Can an object exist in space simply and purely? If landscape, following Denis Cosgrove,[74] cannot exist without its reference to power, economy, and society, and if space, following Henri Lefebvre,[75] is produced, how can we separate out the inherent interrelationships between the myriad causal and resultant meanings associated with landscape and space? How can Judd's objects lack reference to power, economy, or society, and how are they not specifically produced?

In 2010, the Judd Foundation made available online Judd's entire thirteen-thousand-volume library. (Was Judd, maybe, a hoarder?) The website displays pristinely photographed images that take you on a virtual tour of the library space, and each image can then be zoomed in on for closer inspection. By doing so you can see what other volumes surround particular texts, which is important because Judd was quite organized in the way he shelved his books. You may also search the collection by subject, author, or title, providing a scholar of Judd an entirely new opportunity for understanding his mind-set. (The Judd Foundation has also made some archives available to scholars and researchers by appointment.)

It is a curious thought to think of Judd's concept of space in relation to the geographer's concept of space and place. I wondered what geographers, if any, Judd had read during his lifetime, and if they had made their way into Judd's library either before or after his treatise "Specific Objects." Here is what is not included in his library: Yi-Fu Tuan, David Harvey, Mark Augé, Henri Lefebvre, Michel de Certeau, Carl Sauer. The texts of geographic interest in his library are these: John Brinkerhoff Jackson, *The Southern Landscape Tradition in Texas* (1980) and *American Space* (1972); Paul Virilio, *The Aesthetics of Disappearance* (1980); Gaston Bachelard, *The Poetics of Space* (1964). Having studied philosophy, Judd has a healthy number of philosophers represented in his library (484 books on the subject), including the following: Martin Heidegger, *Being and Time* (1962); Immanuel Kant, *The Critique of Pure Reason* (1965); G. W. F. Hegel, *On Art, Religion and Philosophy* (1970) and *Introduction to Aesthetics* (1979).

If Judd was familiar with J. B. Jackson's writing on landscape, then he was aware of how humans have a direct hand in shaping the landscape that surrounds them, and that this landscape—no matter how simple or mundane—is actually quite rich with detail. With this view, he could have potentially looked at Marfa as a landscape of simplicity that actually revealed the beauty of small American towns. Further, in reading Bachelard, he could have made the connection between public and private space, and how our interactions in private space—specifically the space of our homes—are integral to the rest of our experiences with the exterior world. Home is important for Bachelard, just as it is for Judd. This, again, is revealed as you walk through his private spaces in Marfa.

The private spaces of Judd in Marfa are more than just living spaces. The space of home is the first universe that we know, and the layout of these spaces and the practical objects within them define our intimate experiences there.[76] Can you picture the kitchen of your childhood home? What did your mother's cooking smell like? What kind of everyday china did you use? Did you eat cereal or eggs for breakfast? And so on. I can picture all these details and more from my childhood home, and I would imagine that you could picture yours, too. No, you can't go home again, but you sure can remember a lot of your time there, no matter how many years it has been. Why do we spend so much energy and time creating and caring for our homes? Why does a hotel room always feel so stale? Why did Judd constantly move around his furniture and art to rework the spaces that he occupied, in a search for getting it *just right*? We know how important our personal spaces are, whether or not we can articulate why. The inclusion of art in a space gives the entire room more meaningful substance, and the art relates to the chair, which relates to the desk, which relates to the window. "An artist does not create the way he lives, he lives the way he creates."[77]

Being able to see Judd's private spaces offers me insight into his philosophy, and the relationship between these spaces and his work is clear. Judd thought a lot about space, and he wrote that "time and space don't exist; they are made by events and positions."[78] The catalogue of his work—often referred to as "boxes," "stacks," and "progressions"—is ordered, simple, and methodical. His bedrooms, kitchens, and studios are the same. Further, the line that separates the two spaces—work and living, art and life—is no longer a clear division. Judd's life is his work, and his work is his life. This is evidenced as I take a tour of the studios or the Block and see how interwoven his art is to his everyday life. It softens Judd the creator into Judd the human.

Realizing that the links I am making are entirely speculative, I maintain that the issues of art, architecture, geography, philosophy, anthropology, and history are all related, particularly in relation to Judd. That he has the aforementioned texts in his library at least implies that he had read them.[79] What I propose is that Judd's interest in and knowledge of these philosophical areas contributed to his specific writing on art and architecture. Essentially, art cannot be removed from life, placed on a pedestal, and treated as an object alone in the world. And Judd's criticism of the traditional museum describes this. Art is a living history and it exists in living spaces, not stale museum settings. Judd's work in Marfa is the culmination of this idea.

Donald Judd's daughter, Rainer, directed a short film, *Remember Back, Remember When*, from 2008. It's about an artist in a small town in West Texas, but it's never explicit that Judd is the artist and Marfa is the town. I think Rainer's voice is of particular interest, and her very personal film puts Judd in a new light for me. In a film that is just over ten minutes long, the viewer is presented with an account of a marital dispute that ends with the father driving off with his two children crying out in the back of the pickup truck's small cab.

The film takes place in West Texas in 1977. Two young children, a boy and a girl, are playing in the front yard of a modest home in an otherwise unremarkable town. To anyone familiar with Marfa or with Judd's personal history, it's easy to make the assumption that the children represent Rainer and her brother, Flavin; the mother and wife is Julie Finch; and the father and husband is Donald Judd. The children are digging up and moving around dirt in the front yard with plastic trucks and buckets.

The landscape is identifiable as Marfa, and it is no stretch to imagine this space as the late 1970s—it requires very little maneuvering as a filmmaker to refrain from including the modern and refurbished housing of Marfa of recent years. The sun is blinding, as it has always been; the colors are rich and yet sun washed, as they have always been.

The mother, drinking tequila with the father in the middle of the day, makes mention of going back to New York, where the father will be able to access the people who are at present confused by his artistic work. The father grumbles, "Too many people is the problem with New York." The father's refusal escalates with passion; the one attempt at a flirty and playful reconciliation only allows the woman to suggest that her husband is having an affair, which angers him more. The wife asks him not to fight in front of the children. "I don't give a damn who sees the goddamn truth," says the father. Is this Judd talking, or is an older Rainer speaking through him?

The man starts to drive off in his truck, only to stop and reverse back into the yard. He gathers up both children, scared and clinging to their mother, and again the truck takes off down the road. The mother is left standing alone in the yard, upset, confused, and what we can only imagine as a little bit fearful: for her children and for her own uncertain future.

This film serves as a reminder of the realness of the characters in Judd's life. It's unfortunate that he died relatively young, with so much more work to be done. How would Marfa have looked had he had another twenty years there? We are left with this small town as a relic to the artist. His home and studio space are fetishized; nothing has been altered since his death. From the slippers at his bedside, to the stacks of bowls in the kitchen, to the well-ordered and simple piles of drawings and plans in his office, *this* Marfa belongs to the patriarch Judd. How have Rainer and Flavin (and Julie) found their own space outside of Judd's legacy? How does it feel to live with the ghost of this man who is held in such high esteem (if not without anecdotal eccentricity and passion), knowing all too well the details of his flaws?

The modern Marfan, or tourist to Marfa, readily touts its remoteness and simplicity as a continuing draw. This is a romantic notion that is true for few people, or at least, few residents of Marfa. Countless people have moved here in search of simplicity and space, with the idea of freedom from the problems that surround them. In reality, the smallness of Marfa, and perhaps the abundance of space, is exactly what magnifies one's problems. One local dubbed the draw to the town the "Marfa mystique," as if it were an illness that could be treated. "You can't escape your problems here," said another. "You deal with them head on."

Another local spoke of the "Marfa blues," which is something I have experienced after only a couple of months. For me, it could be because of my nature, and my hesitation around large groups. I don't want to go to the busy place; I want to go to the empty place. I don't mind being alone, and I keep myself busy between work and writing and reading. I like that I can be anonymous in Marfa, but I don't want to be antisocial either, and I don't want to be lonely. But, before long and without thinking about it, the isolation can get to me. The mystique pulls you in, and the blues drive you away.

For Rainer and Flavin, their childhood was marked by their parents' divorce and their subsequent move to Marfa. As is usually the case, this did not come without incident. Julie and Don divorced in 1976, but the next year the children were essentially kidnapped from New York and taken to Marfa by their father.[80] Eventually, the family found itself in the charming Presidio County courthouse for the custody battle, and both children chose to stay with their father in Marfa. Rainer's Marfa, then, is a much different place than it is to a newcomer of recent years. *Her* Marfa, though filled with beautiful light, beautiful art, and what at times must be nostalgia for her late father, is also filled with the emotions of a childhood with an impassioned artist and father, and the memory of her parents' failing marriage. Her Marfa is home, but it is also the starting point for a future elsewhere.

Remember Back, Remember When is a narrative based on truth, and the landscape in the story is the landscape in the film. Marfa does not only represent a landscape or an idea; it is one of the characters in the story. As Marfa has become perhaps greater than its parts combined because of its noted isolation, saturation of arts, and the subsequent aura and weight that come with this, it has become a place of meaning outside of its self or space.

Judd wrote that there was unfortunately little concern for old buildings in American towns and cities.[81] Buildings were not built to last, and they were easily torn down in order to build something new. There was no respect for the history of place, as evidenced by the physical structures that composed this place. His transformation of the buildings in Marfa would seem to support his belief that preexisting structures should be worked *with*—even at a cost beyond that of new construction[82]—and that untouched land should remain untouched. However, he also gutted buildings to the bare bones. Was he perhaps erasing history and not revealing it? Despite the credit often given to him as an architectural and landscape preservationist, Judd did want to construct new buildings at Fort D. A. Russell, having initially found the place to be "a wreck."[83] He wrote that, were he to do it all over, "new buildings would have been better,"[84] and this writing conflicts with his stated ideology of preservation.

As the space of the Chinati Foundation stands now, however, I cannot imagine anything but what is presented to me: the refurbished and repurposed use of old space. Judd contradicts himself in his writing, a trait not unique to him. His son, Flavin, put it eloquently in the recent publication of *Donald Judd: Writings* from 2016: "Don's writings are disorganized, scattered, repetitive, and incomplete, and that is as it should be. They are his verbal sketchbook."[85]

I've probably contradicted myself in this writing, because writing is thinking, and thinking is a process of exploring who we are and what we value. The contradictions show an active mind, constantly engaged with his ideas and with his projects in search of something complete and pure and beautiful.

CHAPTER 5

MARFA AFTER JUDD

☐

About one year after Judd's death, the *New York Times* art critic Roberta Smith pondered the future of Marfa and of the Chinati Foundation. "If Marfa is preserved and becomes accessible to the public," she wrote, Chinati "will become one of the most substantial single-artist museums in the world."[1] Marfa has become this accessible place, and Chinati has lived up to Smith's prediction, but this was no overnight sensation. The development of Marfa has come at the hands of various players who built on the work of previous newcomers and locals. In this way the development continues to morph with each year, with each business, and with each new or established local who makes his or her own contribution in whatever form that takes.

Donald Judd's formation of the Chinati Foundation took over twenty years and allowed him to develop his ideas on life and art in a landscape far removed from the art world. Since his death, the museum of his creation and the estate that manages his personal spaces have built on his philosophical and artistic foundations, carving out a place for Judd's legacy in a global cultural network that continues to draw visitors to Marfa, in this way making the town an arts mecca. To experience the places of the Chinati and Judd Foundations is to experience a particular kind of Marfa, and a steady calendar of cultural programming from these and other foundations and businesses continues to draw visitors.

Chinati's Rob Weiner estimates that the foundation received 11,000 visitors in 2011,[2] more than double the estimated number of visitors to the museum in 1995.[3] (Curiously, the Judd Foundation estimates only 2,500 visitors for that same year.)[4] Jenny Moore estimates that Chinati will see 40,000 visitors in 2017. By comparison, the Louvre is the world's busiest museum with 8,500,000 annual visitors.[5] The visitor numbers to Marfa have increased alongside the town's growing exposure to the outside world, and the cultural institutions that infiltrated Marfa since Judd's death have contributed to this growth. A review of incoming residents and new businesses can help navigate and explain the development of Marfa over the last twenty years.

I spoke with Rob in 2011 about the changes as he has seen them develop in Marfa over the course of his decades-long tenure with Chinati. "When did people start moving here?" I asked.

"It wasn't a day. But you can look at certain key developments that you know had an impact, because of Judd's attitudes as an artist and his vision as a sort of cultural totem. He created a museum not just for his own art but also for his selected artists. So it's sort of like other museums but also sort of not like other museums. Judd is there, and the culture then begins to surround him with his assistants, with the curators, with people he employs in the town, with the artists that come to visit the museum. It begins to make its impact because Judd is a pretty influential thinker in his own way. Ripples. We took that idea and turned it into a residency program—artists coming here to make work in Marfa. He always wanted an artist here, and we made sure there was. It still doesn't have particular requirements to it."

Rob spoke of coming to Marfa as an employee of Judd's in 1989. "It was beautiful. All the things that make it alluring and incredible were alluring and incredible in 1989. It was gorgeous, the landscape—hardscrabble. The things that still give it character were there. You saw the attraction right away. Living here was really hard, for me—I had a lot of work. We were so occupied with what we were doing that you didn't take time to feel deprived. It was a much tougher distance because there wasn't much activity at all and the main streets were boarded over, except for the excitement with our projects with Judd, in fixing up all these places. The aluminum pieces were already there, so there was already this incredible reason to stick around and be a part of it. Artists were coming. It was already for me an intoxicating situation."

Tim Crowley, the "patron saint"[6] of Marfa (and referred to by some, perhaps with a different tone, as "King Crowley"), first traveled there to attend Chinati's Open House in 1991.[7] He had gone to law school with a friend and Marfa native, Pablo Alvarado, who owns a home in town and had invited him to visit. Tim and his then wife Lynn were drawn to the landscape of Marfa, and they were also art aficionados—Lynn owned a gallery in Houston. At that time, Marfa's real estate was dirt cheap, and Tim and Lynn no doubt saw the potential of Marfa and the opportunity it presented. Theirs was not unlike Judd's opportunity in the early 1970s: real estate was cheap, businesses were shuttered, and no one else was buying.

Tim and Lynn ultimately purchased dozens of properties and encouraged their friends to come visit and to also purchase real estate. Tim's brother, son, and mother also moved to Marfa.[8]

What is significant about the work of Tim and Lynn is that they financially invested in Marfa's infrastructure—something that Judd had failed to do. While Judd's interest in Marfa was largely in renovating his own spaces (although Rob tells me that he did care deeply for the community and the landscape), Tim and Lynn worked beyond the borders of their home to contribute to the broader community by way of public spaces and local businesses. Judd, at one point the largest employer in Marfa,[9] had discussed expanding beyond his own spaces and harvesting local resources to create jobs and build community. He wanted to bottle and sell local spring water, for example, and was interested in starting a farmers' market for local vendors to sell their homemade goods,[10] but these plans never came to fruition. Tim and Lynn, however, opened the Crowley Theater and the Marfa Book Company and were original investors in renovating the Thunderbird Hotel, among other ventures. In 2016, Crowley opened the Hotel Saint George.

Tim also lent his plot of land on the southwest side of the railroad tracks on South Highland Avenue to the city and built what locals referred to as "the shade structure" in 2007. While the construction of the Hotel Saint George caused some changes to the downtown landscape, including removal of the shade structure, the plan was to ultimately reinstall part of it at another location, as it has been a loved and well-used place by residents and visitors. (It has since been repurposed, but not for community use.) When it first went up, the Judd Foundation matched Tim's donation by allowing him to choose styles of Judd-designed furniture for the space, which were then commissioned and built locally. Tim is neither a geographer nor a philosopher, but there is a geographical sensibility in his decision *not* to formally name this space in any particular way. To give something a name is to assign meaning to it—there is no formal name for the space because the space changes. The shade structure's large covered footprint offered midday breaks from the sun, and its central location offered an excellent gathering point for the community. It was also nice to be able to sit on and use the Judd benches and tables, as it offered another avenue into Judd's work (you can look *and* touch). Whereas the spaces of both Chinati and Judd are hands-off, the outdoor pieces at the shade structure were usable, practical, and unique to Marfa.

In 1999, Tim and Lynn opened the Marfa Book Company and later added a coffee and wine bar[11] to the space. It provided an opportunity for locals and visitors to engage with each other, something that many have credited with fostering community between old and new Marfa. It became an unofficial meeting point, not unlike the post office, and it encouraged extended periods of gathering for its patrons. Tim sold the bookstore to a local, Tim Johnson, who continues to develop community events by hosting writers' and artists' talks and regularly partners with the other local foundations to develop and host programming. In 2001, the Crowley Theater opened in the large space of a former feed store, and it is free for use by nonprofit organizations.

The Crowley Theater, 2017.

In 2000, the Dan Flavin installation, *untitled (Marfa project)*, was finally completed at the Chinati Foundation. Although this would not be the last work to be permanently installed at Chinati,[12] it did mark the conclusion of a dialogue that had begun in 1979 between Judd and Flavin[13] and became one of the cornerstone pieces of the museum.

Notable incoming residents throughout the 1990s included Dick DeGuerin, a criminal defense attorney based in Houston; the artist Charles Mary Kubricht of Houston and New York; and the artist Mary Shaffer, among many others. As best articulated in Marfa's weekly paper in 1997, "The future economic force driving this ranching community will be art-related."[14] These and many other diverse new residents brought a surge of life and activity to Marfa during the 1990s. Most importantly, these newcomers brought money to Marfa, and with that money, renovated homes. And, most of them were from other parts of Texas.

Kubricht's work in particular has been based on her experience of the landscape in Marfa. She looks for "what is hidden in the landscape"[15] and studied military tracking manuals to develop her own seeing skills, often hiking with Border Patrol trackers to practice her optical exercises and learn from their methods. Her work, like Judd's, asks of the viewer an essential component to seeing the work: movement. A 2011 installation at the Marfa Book Company's gallery covered the walls and ceiling with painted black and white geometric shapes. Inspired by dazzle camouflage, a painting technique used on ships during World War I,[16] *The Figure Is Always Ground* was unsettling and transformative. Her work, like that of other artists in Marfa, is notable to me for its complete opposition to the Judd-inspired minimalism that permeates the town.

There are always a number of people in Marfa who are there temporarily to produce creative work. Whether they are inspired specifically by the landscape or are just in need of space and time itself, the place of Marfa directly contributes to the output of artists and writers. And as these artists and writers take their work and experience back to their home cities, they take a piece of Marfa with them, disseminating its culture and marketing Marfa to outsiders. The Chinati Foundation's residency program, started by Judd, has

The Figure Is Always Ground, 2011. Photo by Charles Mary Kubricht.

hosted nearly 150 artists since 1989.[17] Fieldwork: Marfa is a newer residency program run jointly by two foreign schools, ESBA Nantes Métropole and HEAD-Genéve, and is "dedicated to the practice of art in public space, critical approaches to landscape and artistic projects based on field investigation methods."[18] This residency program recently drew 220 applications from thirty-seven countries, which shows how expansive Marfa's cultural placement is. One of the most formative residency programs comes from the Lannan Foundation, "dedicated to cultural freedom, diversity and creativity through projects which support exceptional contemporary artists and writers,"[19] which began purchasing houses in Marfa in 1997 with the intention of starting a writer-in-residence program. By 2001, the foundation was renovating a third house and had purchased two more,[20] and in 2002 it purchased a sixth house.[21] To date the Lannan Foundation has supported over three hundred artists and writers in residence in Marfa.[22]

While in Vermont, I saw a former Lannan resident who had come to speak at the Vermont Studio Center. I told him I had spent time in Marfa and was writing about it. "It's strange," he said, "to be a modest writer with a modest income, and to go to this beautiful place to write and have a six-thousand-dollar Eames lounge chair in your living room. It's excessive. Does a writer do a better job, living in a house that is impeccably designed and decorated? It's all part of the shtick of Marfa. Everything is curated." When he said that, it made me wonder if his time in Marfa had been fruitful.

I think about the many Lannan residents who have cycled through town. They are here for quiet. They are here for space. They are here to write. They are integrated into the small scene in town, but in large part they, like me, spend their days alone, indoors—writing, reading, thinking. In some ways we are taking from Marfa without giving back, which doesn't sit right with me. That said, what is the best way to contribute to the Marfa community, especially as a visitor? I haven't yet figured this out. Many locals feel that the school system is in terrible shape; perhaps contributing to Marfa Independent School District is the best way to help the town. There is also the library and the radio station that rely on outside funding, and both nonprofits are essential to Marfa's community.

After the Lannan Foundation's establishment, other foundations followed suit. The International Woman's Foundation was established in the former officers' quarters of Fort D. A. Russell in 2002 with the intention of supporting female artists.[23] Ballroom Marfa opened in 2003 as a contemporary arts and culture space.[24] Ballroom in one sense disrupted the arts fabric of the community that for years relied solely on Chinati. Chinati and Judd's legend had been the focal points for many tourists, and Marianne Stockebrand, Judd's partner, was reportedly the "queen bee" of town before other organizations opened. With the opening of Ballroom, there was a new kid on the block. With it came a certain level of celebrity, and parties became private, and "things got small," as one resident noted. Ballroom's two founders, Fairfax Dorn and Virginia Lebermann, notably come from two Texas dynasties, what are now known as Brown & Root Industrial Services and the O'Connor Family Ranches, respectively. Chinati had been "so powerful it created division," a local told me, adding that "Ballroom was founded by essentially two professional hostesses," who were looking to do more in Marfa with regard to cultural programming. (The comment was half joking, and if anything, Dorn and Lebermann are professional fund-raisers.) Again, through its new residents, Marfa becomes closely tied to these other places of Texas: Houston, Dallas, Austin.

I spoke with Dorn about the history of Ballroom and its impact in Marfa. She views Ballroom as an attractor, as a conduit for creating energy. Many of the exhibitions are specifically commissioned for Ballroom, not unlike Judd's desire to have an artist come and make something for Chinati. Ballroom invites artists to come to Marfa, be it one or two weeks or one or two months, and to create something inspired by or otherwise focused on Marfa. It's open-ended and has taken many forms.

Besides visual exhibitions, Ballroom Marfa produces film and music events as well as various interdisciplinary symposiums, and for years its leaders were working on a project to build a drive-in theater in Vizcaino Park, on the eastern side of town. (They decided to pull the plug on this project to focus on Ballroom Marfa's programming.)[25] Most of Ballroom's programming is free and open to the public, and they have extended their brand to other cities by holding fund-raisers in New York and hosting the Marfa Dialogues in other cities.

The Ayn Foundation, which is "committed to comprehensive, large-scale projects by major international artists for presentation to the public,"[26] opened its Marfa galleries in 2005, and its two galleries permanently display Andy Warhol's *The Last Supper* and Maria Zerres's *September Eleven*. With a bit of tongue-in-cheek humor, the aptly named Pizza Foundation opened in 2002 to feed all the hungry arts tourists.

Speaking of food, eating well in Marfa can be a challenge. Before the opening of a handful of Marfa restaurants in the early 2000s, the only place available to eat on a Sunday evening was inside the Stripes gas station.[27] That changed with the opening of Jett's Grill, Maiya's, Cochineal, Pizza Foundation, and Food Shark, as well as the coffee-producing Squeeze Marfa and Frama, all of which opened between 2002 and 2008. Now it is possible to get a $32 steak paired with a $16 glass of wine, but the question remains, Who is meant to consume these items? It is the tourist and only some locals who are able to spend this kind of money on dining. While restaurateur Maiya Keck was vocal about her targeted demographic (tourists), other business owners actively sought out local opinion. Dan and Jesse Browning, entrepreneurs who moved to Marfa, asked community members what kind of business they wanted to see open. When locals responded that a laundromat was needed, they listened and opened Frama Coffee and Tumbleweed Laundry, a place where you can do your laundry and grab a latte.

In 2009, the concert space and bar Padre's opened in what used to be a funeral home, and this venue saw a steady flow of musicians through its doors (like many Marfa establishments opened in the 2000s, it has since closed). Playing a show in Marfa "is a mixed blessing for touring musicians."[28] The crowds are small, but the significance of playing in Marfa gives a particular amount of credibility and coolness. As with an artist who participates in a residency or exhibition in Marfa, the association with Marfa in this way is a form of cultural capital. Padre's also offered a democratic venue for natives and tourists alike to gather in a simple but fun, unassuming way. (Live music, Moon Pies, Lone Star draft, and red beans and rice are delightfully about as unassuming as you can get.) Like the bookstore's coffee and wine bar, it was a catalyst that brought many different kinds of people together. One former resident said that both the Frama/Tumbleweed and Padre's "improved town relations" through their simplicity and utilitarianism. As one local poetically articulated to me, "If Padre's wasn't here, I wouldn't go over there and drink beer, but it is, so I do." Amen to that. Or:

If Padre's
wasn't here,
I wouldn't go over there
and drink beer,
but it is,
so
I do.

Now he goes to the Lost Horse, which opened in 2011, for that beer.

This volume of bars and restaurants wasn't needed until the tourists started showing up, and it has mostly been nonnatives who have opened these establishments. So there is a sort of cycle of outsiders coming to Marfa to open up something that continues to cater to outsiders. But the outsiders also bring an irritation to the locals, arriving and asking annoying questions (Why did you move here?), but they are necessary for the success of these now-local businesses. One of the food trucks, upon celebrating four years in Marfa, prefaced its anniversary announcement by writing that it was "really for the locals." Perhaps this is overly sensitive, but to me that comes off as biting the hand that feeds you. Still, I can appreciate wanting a break from the influx of tourists, and perhaps being nostalgic for a time when there wasn't such a scene in Marfa.

Considering the quantity of work being exhibited in Marfa among these various cultural foundations, it is surprising how often the topics exhibited or discussed qualitatively have nothing to do with Marfa's location or identity. The magnificent opportunity created by these foundations is an exploration of local, relevant topics such as water, sustainability, range management, and the border. When exhibits and events do focus on these topics, they are the ones that contribute most significantly to the placing of Marfa in contemporary culture and to situating it as part of Texas.

One example is the Marfa Dialogues, a series of discussions and events put on by Ballroom Marfa. The first Marfa Dialogues in 2010 focused on issues of the border, and the second Marfa Dialogues in 2012 focused on climate change and sustainability. But the last three Marfa Dialogues (2013, 2014, 2016) have taken the show on the road, traveling to New York, St. Louis, and Houston, respectively. This kind of programming literally takes the Marfa brand and transports it to another place. These symposiums provide an opportunity for artists, scholars, and activists to engage in critical discussion and open dialogue, not to mention spreading the mythology of Marfa to other places. That said, it is in Ballroom's best interest to expand its reach outside the space of Marfa, because it doesn't have an endowment and must constantly work to secure funding.

In 2003, the derelict Thunderbird Hotel was purchased and closed for renovations. Its initial patron, Liz Lambert—also from Texas ranching heritage—had already become somewhat famous for her restoration of the Hotel San Jose on South Congress Avenue in Austin. (She has been credited for jump-starting a rejuvenation of residents and tourists to the once-desolate neighborhood.)[29] In 2005, the Thunderbird reopened to great acclaim. The next year, Lambert's next project in Marfa, El Cosmico, broke ground. Perhaps it is her personal history, coming from West Texas heritage, that made her influence on Marfa especially fitting, because she understood the challenges of the landscape. El Cosmico is hard to describe. It is an alternative, fluid campground, with safari tents, teepees, a yurt, and refurbished vintage trailers available to rent. Lambert's goal with El Cosmico is to explore "how to interact with the land gently,"[30] and she views the site as a place of continual change and experimentation. The space of El Cosmico is modest, come-as-you-are, and definitely unique.

The restoration of the Thunderbird, as well as the planning of El Cosmico, allowed for Lambert's collaboration with designers and

El Cosmico's grounds, 2017.

students.[31] Joey Benton, a Marfa local who originally moved there with the future restaurateur Maiya Keck to catalogue Judd's estate in 1994, helped design and build the interior spaces. Jamey Garza and his wife, Constance, who together had designed furniture for the Hotel San Jose, were also invited to design furniture for the Thunderbird, and they moved to Marfa in 2003. While the Garzas originally planned to work on the project and then move on, they ended up staying in Marfa.

The more you get to know Marfa, the easier it is to understand how Benton and the Garzas have kept busy with their custom design work and furniture. Between the new restaurants and businesses that have opened (and closed) and an increase in home renovations, there continues to be a market for their work. By designing and building furniture locally in Marfa for the past ten or twenty years, these designers have, I believe, contributed to the style of Marfa. The Garzas have expanded outside of Marfa to market and sell their work (under the names Garza Furniture Design and Textiles by Constance), which can be found in stores all over the country and even internationally. Benton's business, Silla (Spanish for "chair"), continues to produce furniture and custom work in Marfa and its environs.

Despite the restorations of both the Hotel Paisano and Thunderbird Hotel, there remain limited housing options in Marfa for the temporary visitor. Between the town's six hotels,[32] there are only about 150 rooms, and during any number of busy weekends, the rooms sell out quickly. But the answer is not to build a large chain hotel on the outskirts of town, which would create placelessness. The new Hotel Saint George works because it is unique to Marfa, and it is designed to work with the existing downtown space (although the fact that its four stories make it taller than the courthouse initially upset some locals), but it is also catering to a very specific kind of tourist—the kind who can afford a $28 fish-and-chips special. Tim Crowley was wise to build his hotel locally, because he knew that if he didn't, some chain could eventually come in and install a big ugly mess. But I do wonder if a chain could come to Marfa to build something that does fit in with its character and style. In 2015, Standard International Management (which

Thunderbird Hotel, 2011.

owns The Standard hotels in New York, Miami, and Los Angeles) took a 51 percent ownership of Lambert's Bunkhouse Group (hotels in Austin, San Antonio, and the aforementioned El Cosmico in Marfa).[33] So there might be room to add something more substantial in Marfa.

I think about how the design and space of the Saint George have changed the experience of Marfa, for both visitors and locals. The hotel lobby can be like a different world, and it is now possible to get breakfast, lunch, and dinner every day of the week. Things always seem delightfully bustling at the Saint George. Compared with the still-quiet Marfa town, passing through the hotel's doors feels like entering a larger city. But is it presenting a falsified sense of place? Or has Marfa changed so much that the hotel is actually reflecting this change and catering to the kind of people who are coming to town? This isn't a criticism, and I like the hotel's space. The bar is a great place to people-watch and to meet with a friend for a drink, and it seems like I always greet a new face there. Perhaps this newer space in Marfa is acting as the Marfa Book Company's coffee shop once did: bringing people together.

Cultural productions are rituals, and they take many forms in Marfa. The fact that the quantity and quality of cultural productions are both high in Marfa is testament to the resulting cultural capital. Despite relatively low attendance numbers (when compared to those of a larger city),[34] these activities are important to Marfa's identity and economy. There is a *density* of culture in Marfa, a distillation of good to better, that provides local and visitor alike the opportunity for high-quality activities. In no particular order, here is a sampling of cultural productions that one may experience in Marfa: Trans-Pecos Music Festival, CineMarfa Film Festival, Marfa Film Festival, Chinati Open House Weekend, Marfa Lights Festival, Farm Stand Marfa, lectures at the Marfa Book Company, Ballroom Marfa's free summer DJ Camp for children and teenagers, as well as plays, lectures, talent shows, film screenings, music events, dances, colloquiums, and so on at the Crowley Theater (between 2001 and 2016 there have been over three hundred events there, most of them free).[35] Even the annual citywide yard sale is a cultural production, providing a focused agenda that allows the active participation of citizens and visitors, if not a voyeuristic opportunity to see inside the homes of Marfans.

Going back to Marfa's earliest ranching days, the town has always offered high-quality cultural productions. Marfa had the Palace Theater, which took the place of the former Opera House; the Texas Theater across the street; a drive-in theater at the western edge of town; and a community of ranchers that were well educated, traveled, and lived "Texas large." Despite the significant lull in activities that resulted from the 1950s drought, Marfa has most certainly recovered—partly by way of Donald Judd, but more so recently by a separate surge of new Marfans and their varied interests. This has allowed locals to partake in events that might not exist without the sustainability provided by tourism.

A number of films have been shot in Marfa in recent years, among them: *No Country for Old Men* (2007), *There Will Be Blood* (2007), *Marfa Girl* (2012), and *Far Marfa* (2013). While the former two use Marfa's landscape as representation, the latter two films take place in Marfa. These films, along with *Giant*, have created an opportunity for film tourism to Marfa, which I define as a desire or motivation to visit the filming location of a movie. The film tourist attempts "to connect with their emotional response to a film at the place in which it was set/filmed."[36] Additionally, these films reach different audiences because they are varied—*Giant* is an epic and a classic, *No Country* and *There Will Be Blood* are successful blockbuster films with well-known casts, Rainer Judd's *Remember Back, Remember When* traveled the short film circuit, *Marfa Girl* reached out to the more arty crowd familiar with Larry Clark's controversial work, and *Far Marfa* accessed the independent film industry.

The film culture of Marfa extends to include two film festivals (Marfa Film Festival and CineMarfa) as well as a growing trend to use the landscape of Marfa for magazine and advertising shoots. Marfa On Location[37] is a production company that assists filmmakers, designers, and photographers while in Marfa. Some of the clients include Neiman Marcus, British Vogue, Frye Boots, W Magazine, and Urban Outfitters. Collectively, these films, festivals, and print media project a specific place of Marfa to the outside world. They highlight the landscape of Marfa and increasingly use the landscape and place as a character itself. They place Marfa in the minds of outsiders and embed it in the ideology of place in Texas.

In 2016, Amazon filmed the TV pilot *I Love Dick* in Marfa, based on the book of the same name by Chris Kraus. The show's creator, Jill Soloway, sets the story in Marfa, and even pokes fun at the some-times-elitist world of art and philosophy. (Dick, played by Kevin Bacon, says at one point, "I haven't read a book in ten years. I'm post-idea.") Soloway "is at least partly condemning those who use the town merely as fuel for their artistic pursuits, which is sort of what she herself is doing by setting the show there in the first place."[38]

The Marfa Film Festival has become well known in the global film festival circuit and "celebrates innovation and excellence in film through mindful curation and fostering a relaxed social space."[39] CineMarfa is a nonprofit that was founded to "promote the art and culture of film and filmmaking in Marfa."[40] Both festivals screen between twenty and thirty films each year. CineMarfa is a free festival that "distinguishes itself from other film festivals by emphasizing the intersection between film and visual art,"[41] as well as screening alternative and archival films that typically are not shown in theaters. It also often features work made by Texas artists.

The Marfa Film Festival, on the other hand, charges $550 for a VIP pass and $275 for a general pass for its five-day event. Individual screenings are $15,[42] but local discounts are given. The pricing-out of local residents is not unique to this film festival, but it is worth noting here. Despite the wealth of cultural events offered year-round in Marfa, many can exclude locals who cannot afford to pay a $10 admission fee. As one Marfa local detailed, "If you do not price the tickets so that the locals can be included . . . you will not find Marfa to be as friendly."[43] (Of note is that both Chinati and Judd are free to full-time residents of Presidio, Brewster, and Jeff Davis Counties.) While the influx of festival attendees brings tourism dollars to Marfa, it can also create an atmosphere of exclusion to the insider from the outsider.

As the popularity of these two film festivals grows, so will Marfa's tourism industry. And sometimes Marfa's residents don't know what to make of all these visitors. The music and film festivals have recently given birth to a niche market for the hipster or "festival" aesthetic, which can stand out in a small town. As one young Marfa boy asked during the 2013 Marfa Film Festival, "Why are all these people wearing costumes?"[44] His question was genuine, but it was one of the funniest and most poignant things I had heard.

Beyond film, art, and music, Marfa and its environs offer other experiences for the visitor. The creation of Big Bend National Park and the McDonald Observatory in the late 1930s first provided an official draw of tourism to Marfa and the surrounding area. It was the nature lover, stargazer, or camper who traveled through West Texas, stopping in Marfa along the way. Marfa was not usually a lone destination site at this time, but a component of the larger narrative of the tourist's experience in West Texas. A weeklong trip through the Big Bend might include stops at Fort Davis, Marfa, Alpine, Terlingua, Marathon, Ruidosa, and other places. Each town offered its own slightly different personality, but they remained small towns with small-town identities. Additionally, the historic Fort Davis and Fort D. A. Russell invited the military tourist to the area, as military tourism is its own niche.[45]

The famous mystery lights continue to draw visitors. The formalized viewing center, created in 2003, is both loved and hated in the community. Those who hate it perhaps recognize the absurdity of the structure, that it represents a forced sense of place and a forced draw of tourism. ("It ruined the experience of the lights. Whereas before you would casually pull off the side of the road on your way back from Alpine, now it was this official structure that ruined the charm of the experience.")[46]

The tourist to Marfa is often in search of an authentic experience. The authentic is a "real" experience, wherein getting "off the beaten path" is desired. The tourist in search of the authentic is looking to uncover something the guidebooks don't contain, to meet the locals and get behind the scenes of the community. She is looking for the unique, the unusual. However, the natures of some tourist attractions in Marfa deny this type of experience. The Chinati and Judd Foundation tours, for example, are particular events, with a limited number of people allowed in each group. They start at a certain time and follow a specific path from one place to the next until their conclusion. People on the tours are dependent on the guide as a source of information and, perhaps, inspiration. That's why I've long thought that the best way to tour the spaces of either foundation is to do so during Open House Weekend. While the massive onslaught of visitors makes this annual weekend in October arguably the worst time to experience Marfa in general, it is the only time that both foundations open their doors for visitors to guide themselves throughout the collection and spaces. In this way, visitors may experience the art and the space at their own pace at their chosen time, making for a much more authentic experience of the art.

What separates Marfa from other places of tourism is that its visual landscape is removed from its placement as a tourist site. By this I mean that there are no rides, no shopping districts, and no guided tours (beyond those of Chinati and the Judd Foundation). Few official markers guide tourists through an agenda, so they must write their own agenda. Perhaps it is this unassuming quality of Marfa that is what its tourists find so appealing as they continue to make the journey. ("I just heard about it and was curious.") When visitors come to Marfa, as one local put it, "They either get it, or they don't." It's very nearly that simple. At first glance, Marfa seems like a sleepy town. And, in fact, on many days of the week there are *not* a lot of things going on. A native in Marfa once remarked to me with some frustration, "They come to Marfa, and I don't know what they do—they walk up and down the street."

Tourists also seek to capture aspects of their experience. While tourists may be innocently photographing in an attempt to document their time in Marfa, they are also participating in the creation of what Edward Said termed "imaginative geographies."[47] The exportation of photographs and imagery, magazine and newspaper articles, blog posts, Instagram, Twitter feeds, and so on over time contribute to a heightened—and false—sense of place. Although by definition tourism means *any* travel outside of one's home (business travel or to see family, etc.) it is generally understood that tourism is centered on pleasure and personal travel. The tourist is interested in experiencing something outside of his or her everyday life; he wants to get away from what is normal or expected. And despite the fact that locals may be participating in what would be normal activity to the tourist when she is at home, away from home any mundane activity becomes different. In this way the tourist places an emphasis on the specialness or significance of events and experiences of the destination site. There is a heightened sense of curiosity and interest by way of the site's inherent otherness. Marfa is different, therefore it is special, and the tourist gazes upon Marfa through this focused lens.

Looking at Marfa through the lens of the tourist camera—specifically on Flickr but also on other social media sites—defines a very specific place. The images work to export Marfa to the outside. The images captured are similar in their subject matter, if varied in the kind of editing or filtering done to them, and a search for "Marfa" on Flickr or Google Images will return thousands of images. Go ahead, do a search now. In fact, I'll do one with you. The subject bar at the top of the Google search returns for me five themes: Hipsters, Lights, El Cosmico, Art, and Donald Judd.

I think about these themes in relation to Marfa, and to be honest, they're not wrong. Currently, this is exactly what defines the place of Marfa, and anyone with Internet access can "see" Marfa by perusing these images. But as someone who feels like she has gotten to know Marfa, I can't help thinking how limiting these themes are (and "Hipsters" is at the very least a loaded term). What's more, they build up Marfa as a very specific place in the mind of the tourist. Marfa isn't alone here. Tourists travel to places that are not their home, and project onto these sites a surface-level understanding of culture, community, geography, and so on. I do this myself, despite my attempts to learn about a place before I go there, and I think it's only human to find ourselves guilty of this: it has been said before me that "we are all tourists."[48]

Today, people seem to be so hyperaware of themselves as tourists and outsiders that they search for the authentic experience even at the cost of sounding absurd. In May 2016, someone posted a listing on Marfa's own version of Craigslist, marfalist.org:

My Google Image search results, July 2016.

I'm planning a random trip with a friend to Marfa in a few weeks. I was hoping to gather anyone's personal suggestions through this message board. We like old buildings, beer, art, music, and meeting people. A recent adventure we were on included enjoying a beer with a 70 year old Australian woman [in] Miami at 3 a.m. Ironically, the beer we shared was Foster's.

The writer is searching for experiences and stories, but setting out to have a "random" or "ironic" experience seems inauthentic to me. It is as if the idea of experience of place must include something absurd or humorous to qualify it as authentic. Of course, not all visitors to Marfa take this approach.

"I think a lot of people come to Marfa thinking they know what they're getting themselves into, but they didn't necessarily do their homework," a friend tells me one night after dinner.

She continues, "It is atypical that Judd and Chinati are public art spaces but you can't just show up to visit. Businesses have strange hours. Unfortunately, I saw a lot of people leave Marfa with a bitter taste in their mouth because they didn't prepare. They would be here for one day, always on a Monday and they'd be like 'What should we do?'"

We laugh about the fact that people do always seem to show up on a Monday, for one day, not knowing that nearly everything is closed that day.

"People leave and they're frustrated and they're mad at Marfa as if it's some sort of entity."

Marfa does feel like an entity to me, because of the press surrounding it and because of this incessant "coolness" factor that seems to permeate every article.

"Marfa has been getting all this press and in certain ways it's cool. The *New York Times* list of places to see before you die [from 2016]—it's an unbelievable context in which to throw Marfa.[49] And of course we're not talking about a long-form article—this is in blurb form. They are expecting something that is more in line with their own tastes and their own expectations of luxury, especially when you put it in between these places to see like Ibiza and Cannes."

I double-check later—Marfa is actually listed (at 48) between Thessaloniki, Greece, and Ubud, Indonesia. It is, still, an incredible sandwich.

"People just come with expectations and no plans and that's a dangerous combination for any place you would go, let alone this place."

I think that some people do have a plan: the plan is not to have a plan. The plan is to have some crazy and wonderful and Instagram-able experience—all by chance. It's some kind of head-scratching search for the authentic, and maybe these visitors think they can take certain liberties in order to achieve this.

"People come here and they treat this town like a sound stage. And they'll ask you the strangest questions like, 'Where do you live?' Why would I tell you my address? There's this weird effect that people get when they visit here and they are so divorced from reality and it allows them to ask invasive questions."

Her comments make me think of the word "spectacle," but before I can say anything, she's already met my thought.

"You're a spectacle here. As soon as you've been asked so many times . . . it becomes performative; you really don't want to talk anymore. You start to resent the questions. They become faceless tourists because they ask the same thing day in and day out."

There's somewhat of a dance here between the local and the tourist, and this is not unique to Marfa. Just as the tourist gazes upon Marfa, the local will direct a gaze back on the tourist. It is a reaction to being gazed at. Although the tourist and the local somewhat depend on each other (the tourist depends on the local for an authentic experience, and the local depends on the tourist for economic success), to be the subject of either gaze is certainly not desirable, at least not explicitly. This is why the tourist's gaze on the local causes a reaction of viewing the tourist with contempt or indifference. To be "a tourist" is not a good thing because it is directly related to the false sense of place garnered through mass tourism. Nobody wants to be a tourist, myself included. We want to be an insider. And maybe this is why people show up without a plan. If you have an unplanned experience, it may feel more authentic.

The people of Marfa are well aware of how their town's popularity as a tourist destination has affected their lives. One remarked, "I am protective of this town," and another noted that she would "prefer that Marfa be a small community." The challenge for locals continues to be finding a balance between preserving Marfa and allowing or even encouraging it to evolve. With the success of tourism in Marfa, the town must react to its changing identity, which changes the experience of place for both its residents and its visitors. And while the outsider dollars provide economic benefits, tourism brings plenty of cultural and social implications.

Someone keyed the new car of a local who had parked it outside of Jett's Grill, and residents have recently complained about things being stolen from unlocked cars. I was completely stunned that this would happen in Marfa, where everyone still leaves their house doors unlocked.

"Welcome to the new Marfa," was the local's response.

Residents have voiced their disapproval of the changes in housing, as each restored and flipped home brings with it rising property taxes.[50] As Marfa's popularity has increased, so have the taxes and appraisal values for residences. Buying a home is simply not an option for many locals. Some locals are able to stay in town thanks only to lower tax rates through homestead and disability exemptions that the county adopted in 2016.[51]

The issue of permanent housing is also a major problem for those who work in Marfa, for the Village Farms hydroponic tomato farm, Presidio County, or the Border Patrol, for example. Many Border Patrol agents commute from Fort Davis or Alpine, and they have limited options when it comes to renting over the long term. Most second-home owners would rather hedge their bets by using sites like Airbnb or VRBO to rent out their spaces, charging anywhere from $77 for a trailer to $775 for a four-bedroom home per night. This may be great for a short-term visitor, but the prices can be detrimental to a local.[52] Rent for a studio or one-bedroom apartment in Marfa currently runs about $700 per month, which can be unaffordable to many residents. (The median income from 2014 is about $42,000 and the median home price is about $113,000.)[53]

The success of Marfa is essentially a catch-22 for its residents, who lament the lack of funds for smaller local needs in the face of outsider grants and funding given to the nonprofit foundations. One local woman hates the fact that streetlights were shut off in 2008 to save the city the $3,126 monthly electric bill, and says that Marfa "needs more things besides art." Marfa may very well need things besides art, but it is beholden to the economic benefits that come with this art.

Those who have tried recently to create more housing in Marfa have failed. In 2005, the now-closed American Plume and Feather factory attempted to build an 88-unit subdivision on its property just south of town and was heavily fought by Marianne Stockebrand. The community divided into two groups: those who wanted to conserve the landscape, and those who wanted to see more housing made available. Those who dislike Judd's *15 untitled works in concrete* at the Chinati Foundation threw Marianne's defense of the landscape back at her. The concrete pieces, says one local, "are purposely alien to the environment"[54] and are no different from a proposed subdivision in the impact on the aesthetic pleasures of Marfa's landscape. Here I have to defend Marianne. Putting in a bland subdivision on the outskirts of town would detract from Marfa's landscape and is what makes placelessness. There is a way to build housing that doesn't detract from the aesthetics of Marfa, but it's admittedly hard to reach a consensus on what that is.

It is understandable that Marfa locals want affordable housing and convenient access to shopping and services. But is building a subdivision or putting in a Wal-Mart (which has been proposed) on Marfa's existing open space going to add more services than it would subtract from Marfa's beauty? It is entirely dependent on personal opinion and priorities. If this type of infrastructure were to arise, then the landscape of Marfa would change, and eventually, possibly, the attraction to Marfa would diminish, because the very place of Marfa would change. The success of Marfa's development in the last twenty years is the result of "a careful preservation of the past while insisting on the highest standards for the future."[55] And while community members may not always agree with these high standards, they are necessary for the preservation of the fabric that defines Marfa. The alternative, for many natives, is a Marfa that was not affected by Judd, not affected by the cultural changes after Judd. A Marfa without Judd or his disciples, however, is a ghost town. I have found that most locals, reluctantly at times, agree with this sentiment. But they still don't want it to become another Santa Fe.

I stopped by a friend's house to discuss Marfa one afternoon. He has since moved away, but at the time he lived in a wonderful bungalow on the northwest side of town, with a large yard and an enviable seating area on the back porch. He was having a rather unsuccessful go at growing tomatoes in the front yard, but he seemed determined and happy enough to be able to adopt such a hobby. We talked about the incessant comparison that outsiders make of Marfa to Santa Fe.

"People always want to compare Marfa to Santa Fe," he tells me. "What's similar is, there are three distinct cultures here—ranchers, Hispanics, and the art mafia. But also economically this has become similar to Santa Fe."

"How do you mean?"

"Economically, everyone has to have three jobs. Either you have no job and a new car, three jobs and no car, or three houses and seven cars and you're here three weeks out of the year. That is Marfa—it's incredibly impoverished, and the home prices are just insane."

"So how does Marfa sustain this?"

"Well, it's not sustainable. It was cheap here once, but it's not cheap here now. Finally housing prices are dropping a little bit. Most people are holding on because they don't want to lose money. It's so expensive to do anything here."

He's right. I think of my recent trip to the Get Go, the well-stocked and premium-priced independent market.

One bag of carrots (organic)
One loaf of bread (whole grain)
One jar of jam (the kind in the charming glass jar
    with a gingham lid that is endlessly reusable)
One jar of peanut butter (organic, creamy)
$20

"The hard thing for me is the food ingredients and fresh meat. All the grass-fed beef that you see on Pinto Canyon Road gets trucked to Tucson and comes back frozen. You can take a cow to Sul Ross and get it slaughtered and split it with someone. And then you have to have somewhere to put it. There isn't a humanely raised chicken to be found for sale."

Despite all this, he's happy in Marfa. He's happy with his tomato garden, and he's happy getting to know people. He does some free-lance writing, but he's not one of the people with three jobs.

"I'm busier here than I ever have been. There's more going on here. So for all that, it is a much richer place. This is a much more diverse, rich place in a lot of ways than Austin, which was a shock. The art world in Austin felt tiny and tight-knit. Here it's a free-for-all in a lot of ways. I certainly see more people here than I did in Brooklyn. No one stopped by in Brooklyn. It's not that hard here, which I like a lot.

"But this is not really sustainable," he continues. "Judd wrote that Marfa is a dying town, but it doesn't deserve to die. There is so little you can do that is truly sustainable. There are not enough people here to consume anything you can do here, so you have to figure out something you can do to capitalize on the Marfa name."

He's right about that. I think of all the makers in Marfa and what kind of products they are making. (There's the Cobra Rock Boot Company, Marfa Brands soap and glassware, Cast + Crew's powder-coated horseshoes in bright colors, jewelry made from pennies flattened by a passing train, and so on.) These makers might not like the suggestion that they are capitalizing on the Marfa name, but I don't think it can be denied that the association with Marfa, whether it is intentional or not, is there.

"The impact of Chinati and Judd is huge. And you can sort of measure it by the housing stock, the restaurants. You look at the Border Patrol. You never see them out. They're either living out of town, [or] they're buying everything at Stripes. Not much of their dollar sticks around. Everything is here because of Judd. This would be Valentine without him. Without Judd, none of these houses get fixed up. People wouldn't come from Austin, Dallas to live here."

We talk about the locals and transplants who maybe aren't interested in Judd, who don't make the connection to what Marfa has become for them.

"The anti-Judd thing is interesting. I think it even exists in the younger, hipper crowd. You never hear of an acknowledgment of his birthday or death day. I'm not saying have a parade, but I think that people forget how absolutely critical his presence was. He really thought about sustainability and how to make this place be somewhat viable. The Border Patrol has no idea what Chinati is, and that's a cultural thing, too. There's not a lot of crossover, but there is certainly some. I don't sense any animosity. The sad thing for me is . . ." He pauses. "Even if you don't care about the importance, the theory or whatever. If you don't appreciate visually what exists here—that's too bad. If you've never experienced anything else, you would have no context. When you hear the principal of the school say . . . he said something on the radio about art not being really important. If you just look at the percentage of employment . . . it's mostly arts related. So here's this guy dismissing the arts as being unimportant." (I tried, unsuccessfully, to find the interview.)

In short, even though Chinati is no longer the only show in town, its popularity and Judd's vision have enabled a new kind of environment in Marfa that is not at all dependent on the arts. Without the arts, however, Marfa as it is, for better or worse, would not exist.

Today, the name Marfa is synonymous with culture, and while this culture has expanded beyond Judd's influence, it remains ultimately reliant on his historic significance. Having said that, Marfa is no longer just about Judd, and some newcomers to Marfa may have no knowledge of his work. They come for other reasons now—to work at the radio station, perhaps, or to retire to the beautiful landscape and enjoy the pleasures of small-town life—and their influence over the past twenty years has also contributed to the sustainability and identity of Marfa.

The new factors of Marfa's culture have also contributed to increased property values, higher taxes, and higher rents, and there are varying opinions in the community on how best to alleviate what is a financial burden to many. The success of Marfa as a place of interest has also created its challenges, but a Marfa without its cultural foundations, their programming, and the accompanying media attention is perhaps a desolate community. One attraction to Marfa may remain the same: the vast, beautiful, perhaps desolate landscape, coupled with the incredible light. But Marfa's future will continue to be reliant on its growing economy of tourism, and the balance that its community members can manage between this and their own needs as a small town.

CHAPTER 6

CONCLUSION

☐

As word of mouth has grown about Marfa, newspaper and magazine articles have slowly but steadily started to add to its identity and attract visitors, who are curious to see for themselves this strange small town in West Texas. A timeline can be drawn of important media attention and events that continue to shape Marfa's cultural importance to an outside world, and further, this information can be related to housing and tax information. Together, these data point to significant growth in Marfa in the time since Judd's death in 1994.

I've read, watched, or listened to every piece of media focused on Marfa going as far back as 1983. These media range from magazine, newspaper, and radio to online journals discussing art, tourism, the environment, the border, the mystery lights, and so on. I've compared the number of media pieces to a timeline of important events in Marfa's history, ranging from local business and foundation openings (Marfa Book Company, Ballroom Marfa, etc.) to major or significant events (the Redford killing, the completion of the Dan Flavin piece at Chinati, etc.). The little written about Marfa in the 1980s and early 1990s mostly made mention of the mystery lights or local politics, following the peak in the attention given to Marfa after Judd's death in 1994. Tourism started to become more the focus beginning with the early 2000s. Today, the writing on Marfa is a combination of many components centered on the town as a destination.

In the past twenty years, Marfa's identity has dramatically evolved. What started with Judd's vision of a unique museum in this remote oasis has led to the small town's acclaim as an internationally recognized place of art and culture, set amid a backdrop of beautiful landscape and incredible light. The irony is perhaps in the popularity of Marfa itself as a destination, for the appeal of Marfa to the masses has no doubt created a steady catalyst for change, welcomed or not. The more that Marfa changes, the further it arguably gets from its original appeal, not only to Donald Judd but to every other native or newcomer who has lived and witnessed the changes taking place in Marfa in recent years. That being said, locals are often quick to acknowledge that Marfa's sustainability is due in large part to these very changes. Based on an understanding of who the person Donald Judd was, it is not without reason to speculate that he would have hated what Marfa has become. Would he have wanted the Robert Irwin piece to continue after realizing that the original hospital building must be torn down? Would he have supported a four-story hotel on South Highland that dwarfs one of his buildings across the street? Would he have been satisfied to be a celebrity in Marfa and be unable to go anywhere unnoticed?

Perhaps, after acknowledging that he had "put Marfa and Presidio County on the art-world map,"[1] he would have retreated to one of his ranches outside of town[2] and secluded himself, or moved on to other projects that took him away from Marfa and Texas altogether.

Who is to say that Marfa has become the place it is, not in spite of but because of Judd's death? During his time in Marfa he was "not politically active, wasn't embraced, and was thought to be eccentric."[3] Of Judd's death, Rob Weiner remarked to me, "The town became something else as a result."[4] Dan Flavin's contributing piece and cornerstone to the museum's collection may never have been completed had Judd been alive, because the two had stopped speaking. The Chinati Foundation now runs on grants and donations and not the largesse of the artist himself, as it had during his lifetime.[5] Sometimes it is in death that a different sort of reverence to an artist and his work can blossom.

By way of the establishment and mission of the Judd Foundation, Judd's studio and living spaces have become fetishized, and his personal spaces are presented not as living, changing spaces but as stagnant, frozen ones. As one Marfa artist aptly described to me, the Chinati Foundation is not a contemporary museum—it is a historical museum presenting "the vision of Donald Judd."[6] True, the most recent Irwin piece challenges this idea, but are there any other artists that Judd would have liked to have produced work for Chinati? Will they be tapped to ensure Chinati's future relevance in the contemporary scene? (Yes, Jenny Moore believes that there is still more work that Chinati can do, both with Judd's own work as well as that of other artists, but it is a finite list and it certainly won't happen overnight.)

Today, the spaces of Marfa removed from Judd are contrastingly very much alive, changing at the hands of other artists and community members. Where Marfa's transformation began with Donald Judd's vision, the work of later residents, particularly Tim Crowley and Rob Weiner but also countless other members of the community, native and not, has ultimately contributed to a newer, modern vision of Marfa. Crowley "gave us a place to be cool. He gave us a place to hang out, he brought his rich friends, he invested money," says one local.

The more Marfa has become recognized as a tourist destination, be it via film, nature, art, or mystery lights, the further it gets from its ranching heritage—but this kind of heritage had already been harming the landscape for many years, and continuous cycles of drought do not help. Many locals readily admit that ranching has become more a side hobby and that the old-timer ranchers are "all dead or dying." In reviewing Marfa's history, it seems that change has always been the conduit that allowed the town's sustainability—first with the ranchers, then with the military, now with the art. The changes that have taken place both economically and culturally in Marfa in the last twenty years have allowed it to sustain its economy without a direct dependence on the productivity of the land, and this has fostered a community-wide recognition of landscape and landscape preservation that permeates the town's culture. This is evidenced by the growing body of cultural productions that focus on these topics and the community's desire to keep the landscape of West Texas intact. (The community has rallied to keep away an increased number of air force bomber routes through the area and a proposed radioactive waste dump in Sierra Blanca, although they have all but lost the battle against the Trans-Pecos natural gas pipeline.)[7] Along with these various economic changes to its recent history, Marfa has also been home to various cultural identities within the community: what's left of the ranchers, the predominant Hispanic population, the artists and makers, the retirees, and other workers. These residents cohabit in a small-town setting, and their interests and activities often, but not always, allow them to cross paths. History will tell what kind of place Marfa will be in another twenty years, but its geographic remoteness and placement near the border will continue to affect its culture and community.

As I've researched the artists and designers who have come to be associated with Marfa, I've often wondered whether or not they share similar beliefs as Donald Judd or if they have taken an entirely different path in their work. The foundations in Marfa and the global influence of Donald Judd's place here have come to signify the place of Marfa as one of clean, minimal lines, and this has been reflected in the architecture and design produced here. Likewise, the consumable work produced in Marfa is a reflection of its identity, and as it is dispersed into the outside world, it carries this meaning. When we purchase something that we believe to be beautiful, that fits with our own aesthetic, we also impose on the work the placing of its origin, which becomes a part of the work. We don't just buy a dress; we buy a hand-embroidered Oaxacan dress from the place of its origin in Mexico. It is this kind of authenticity that makes the physical, commercial object special to us.

The impact of souvenirs and of items specifically purchased in a particular place should not be overlooked.[8] These items, whether large or small, expensive or cheap, convey a sense of place. They are physical tokens of experience and they convey place and memory.

When we purchase something in Marfa, we invest in our belief that Marfa is a special place, one where the environment is (presumably) inspirational to its creators. The work of these various creators is then dispersed beyond Marfa's borders, and carries with it the meaning of Marfa. With Marfa's constantly expanding and shifting identity into a place of tourism and a place that provides cultural capital, this dispersal of identity and goods includes the commodification of Marfa. Beyond the idea of the landscape, there is also now an association of the name Marfa and what that culturally means to the town as a place.

Businesses in Marfa, whether intentionally or not, contribute to the branding of Marfa, and collectively they have been able to disperse the idea of Marfa to the outside world—not to mention sustain their own commercial and private ventures. The modern and beautiful furniture designs of Jamey and Constance Garza represent the place of Marfa. I've spoken with them about their history in Marfa, and, like Judd's work at Chinati, nothing was really planned or mapped out for them. Instead, the evolution of their time in Marfa was organic. What was supposed to be one job became a larger project, which led to another project, which led to another project. But they had wanted to produce their own pieces that anyone could buy, that could be purchased in Marfa or could be taken outside of Marfa. And they worked really hard.

They even had to fight another business that had stolen their designs, producing ever so similar pieces and being sold under a different name, in a different city. This shows that their work is desirable and valuable and, by extension, that Marfa is desirable and valuable. The demand for their products is also a demand for a piece of this Marfa style, a piece of Marfa itself.

The material quality of the products developed in and in the name of Marfa have more to do with the sign they convey and less to do with their actual functionality.[9] Just as *Prada Marfa*'s creators wanted their work to be associated with the name and place of Marfa (without actually installing the work *in* Marfa), other artists, designers, and brands have done the same. "Made in Marfa" is a desirable label, but not all products require this authenticity. While some products carrying the Marfa name are authentically made *in* Marfa (such as Ginger Griffice's Marfa Brands soap), others merely co-opt the name for branding (such as the UK-based *Marfa Journal*).[10] Each time this is done, the branding of Marfa becomes that much further embedded in a certain style, but not embedded in the actual Marfa.

Madewell, a lifestyle and clothing company owned by J.Crew, released in its 2013 summer catalogue two versions of "the Marfa Bag." One is a bucket purse with a Mexican-inspired print on tan leather, and the second is a rectangular, darker tan leather purse with minimal detail. They both have a "found-at-the-flea-market vibe" (sold for $118 and $135, respectively),[11] and both feature a zigzag imprint on parts of the leather. The bags are marketed to women, and they are not made in Marfa—not even made in the United States. Can you picture what they might look like without seeing them? The Marfa Bag appropriates the style of Marfa, but it also perpetuates and builds on the same Marfa style from which it takes. Thanks to the mass-market reach of the Madewell brand, the use of the name Marfa in these two handbags undercuts what the actual people of Marfa do to create and maintain their unique identities. Further, anyone purchasing one of these bags who may or may not have heard of Marfa has bought into the commercialization of the name. They have absorbed the idea of the Marfa identity without actually needing to experience the place.

Some of the products that use the Marfa name are not as authentic as others, meaning they are not handmade or they are not made in Marfa, but they do contribute to the identity of Marfa and its placing to the outside world. Pure Marfa was an online-only website whose offerings were curated to "represent the vibe of Marfa" as defined by "clean lines, rough textures and raw materials" (website no longer available). Mid Century Marfa[12] sold vintage clothing online and used to inhabit a small space above the Tumbleweed Laundry, but then moved to Lockhart. Other stores currently open in Marfa, including Freda[13] and Mirth,[14] curate goods that ostensibly reflect the style and place of Marfa. Local Marfa artists make many of the goods sold in these stores, while some goods are imported from Mexico, and others may have nothing directly to do with Marfa. Cast + Crew sold refurbished mid-century pieces and powder-coated horseshoes ("previously worn by horses in the West Texas region"), some boasting a "Marfa red (Neon)" color that delightfully pops against the landscape. Cast + Crew started as an online store, but its brick-and-mortar presence in Marfa changed how its pieces convey to the consumer—it becomes a part of the style of Marfa by way of its placement.

Perhaps it is the ironic, if not insulting, *Prada Marfa* that speaks best to the high level of class in Marfa that is in contrast to so much of its actual (real) identity. In the ten years since I first came to Marfa, I've seen restaurants and shops open and close with such regularity that it's hard for me to understand why people can take such risks in opening a business in a small town.

While the shop owners have the best of intentions, the smallness of Marfa, despite its tourism draw, seems to limit the number of stores and restaurants that can succeed here.[15] Maintaining a business that caters to outsiders by selling nonessential items is a risky operation, and when compared to the list of business *not* available in Marfa (dentist, dry cleaner, and until 2016 there had not been a pharmacy in Marfa for twenty years), it is perplexing to see a store selling pottery when that might not be what is necessarily needed by the residents.

Besides the straightforward commercial ventures in Marfa, a wealth of cultural productions seek to investigate design, architectural, environmental, and political issues in Marfa and in the greater Big Bend region. Symposiums such as Design Marfa[16] and the Marfa Dialogues[17] create an opportunity for these larger discussions to take place, and Marfa's environmental factors and geographic placement near the border almost demand it. These types of location- and place-based events take the brand Marfa and turn it into a catalyst for change. A community engaged with relevant issues, like land and water use or border issues, will define its very space through the production of these events, which will continue to make the cultural identity of Marfa that much richer.

In 2016, the coffee table book *Marfa Modern* was released, showcasing twenty-one homes in and around Marfa. The photography is beautiful, and the homes are enviable for their spaciousness and seemingly perfect interior designs, but I wonder how this kind of representation serves to undermine Marfa. Those who will look at this book before venturing to Marfa may be in for a surprise, because this book does little to portray what the majority of Marfa homes actually look like. That said, who am I to say that someone's home, portrayed in this book, isn't real to them? These homes are real spaces, as every home in Marfa is a real space. But this kind of book fails to portray the diversity of Marfa's spaces and, in turn, its people.

The challenge for Marfa as a community is finding a balance between the products and ventures that use the town's popularity and culture for self-promotion and the authentic sense of place. "When a town becomes a product and not a vision you lose something."[18] Can Marfa protect itself *from* itself? In the summer of 2013, an installation gave the community of Marfa the opportunity to show that it can.

Some eight years after *Prada Marfa*'s installation, a new sculpture appeared on Route 90, the highway that leads into Marfa from the west. This sculpture represented the modern Marfa, the Marfa that is a style and a brand, and its creator was more than willing to take part in the spectacle. Called *Playboy Marfa*, the installation's three elements—a simple concrete box-like structure, a 1972 Dodge Charger painted entirely matte black, and a large white neon sign—make a clear connection to the core artists of the Chinati Foundation: Donald Judd, John Chamberlain, and Dan Flavin. What was most noticeable about this installation, however, was the shape of its neon sign—the very recognizable "bunny" logo of Playboy—that was nothing more than an advertisement for the brand. *Playboy Marfa* was commissioned and paid for by Playboy.

The installation, designed by Richard Phillips, was approved by Presidio County and put in place over the course of a couple of days in July 2013. Unlike *Prada Marfa*, *Playboy Marfa* was actually in Marfa, at the edge of town just past the cemeteries. Rightfully

Playboy Marfa, 2013.

guessing that Playboy was up to something controversial, the *Big Bend Sentinel* broke the story before the company's formal press release.[19] Marfans had hoped, or at least I did, that the installation was going to mean something more than it did, and for a few weeks in the summer of 2013 it was the talk of the town. Unfortunately, the press release[20] revealed that Playboy's interest in co-opting these three artists of the Chinati Foundation (and by extension, Marfa) was no more than an effort to reinvigorate the brand: it was simply an advertisement. The silver lining to this advertisement's dark cloud was its temporariness; the plans specified it would be up for one year.[21] However, the locals' immediate criticism of the piece prompted its removal in November.

The community's rejection of *Playboy Marfa* took hold when the local Lineaus Lorette filed a complaint with the Texas Department of Transportation almost immediately following its installation, citing the sculpture as advertisement. However, the agency had already come to that conclusion.[22] The neon bunny was a corporate logo and thus in violation of the Highway Beautification Act of 1965, which was created to limit outdoor advertising and billboards along America's highways.[23] It's fitting to mention that this act came about through Texas's Lyndon B. Johnson, but he had been motivated in large part by his wife, Lady Bird, who led much of the effort.[24] The Texas DOT deemed the sculpture illegal advertising and gave Playboy forty-five days to remove it. Playboy wouldn't budge, even though by that point the media attention given to the piece had already given the corporation what it had been after all along—press and advertisement. What's more, *Prada Marfa* was dragged into the battle, as it had also been cited by the Texas Department of Transportation as an illegal advertisement.[25] And so both installations' fates became unknown.

The forced removal of either would put a new spin on each installation and, perhaps more importantly, on the status of Marfa as a cultural center. Playboy's attorney in the case happens to be a part-time Marfa resident, Dick DeGuerin, who said that *Playboy Marfa* is "provocative, yes, but a contribution to the overall art scene in Marfa."[26]

"Kill the Bunny" sticker by Julie Speed, 2013.

The battle ultimately showed that, to Marfans, there is a fine line between a contribution to and a desecration of place. Perhaps *Playboy Marfa* was merely the straw that broke the camel's back, prompting much of the community to reject it. (The local artist Julie Speed created stickers with the bunny logo in crosshairs that said "Kill the Bunny.")

The Texas Department of Transportation ordered Playboy to remove the installation, which happened in November 2013. It was then transferred to the Dallas Contemporary, where it was installed as part of a 2014 show of Richard Phillips's work.[27] Also in 2014, Texas DOT declared *Prada Marfa* a "museum site," thus saving it from the wrecking ball.[28]

Whereas the works of the Chinati Foundation, from which Phillips drew his inspiration, are permanent, site-specific pieces, *Playboy Marfa* was dismantled and then reinstalled outside of Marfa. It is not permanent, not site-specific. It meant something entirely different when installed in Dallas. *Playboy Marfa* became a metarepresentation of Marfa, co-opting its landscape and art but removed from the source materials' inspiration and meaning. It took the place of Marfa outside of Marfa and situated it in a distant museum as a spectacle.

Does the removal of *Playboy Marfa* signal the limit of the amount of exploitation Marfa residents can take? What does it say that residents were so quick to despise *Playboy Marfa*, but equally quick to defend *Prada Marfa*? I asked Lineaus Lorette what he thought the difference was between the two installations.

"The difference is smut, sexism. It was the religious aspect of it."

But could it also have been the fact that *Playboy Marfa* was on the doorstep of town, unlike the farther-away *Prada Marfa*? I honestly think it was partly a factor of time. When *Prada Marfa* was installed, Marfa had not yet become the place that it is now, "a destination on the world hipster tour," as described to me by Lorette. If *Prada Marfa* were to be proposed today, a mere ten years after it was installed, would the community embrace it? Or would they reject it like they did the Playboy piece? Whatever the case, *Playboy Marfa* is gone now, and *Prada Marfa* stands.

Throughout this writing I have traced the evolution of Marfa from its earliest days of ranching and the building of the railroad to its contemporary identity as a cultural hotspot. The identity of Marfa is today reliant on the work of Donald Judd, who built an alternative museum there, but the real story of Marfa in many ways begins in the post-Judd era with the arrival of newcomers and nonprofit foundations, in addition to the restaurants and stores that help define the Marfa experience. These new members of the community have allowed Marfa to further evolve into a place of art, music, film, and, by way of these features, tourism. As opposed to other cities that continue to grow in size and numbers, Marfa's population has hovered at two thousand for the past fifteen years, and it is not expected to change any time soon. Marfa's geography, its placement in West Texas in the dry and harsh terrain of the Chihuahuan Desert, will protect it from too much growth.

Small towns can be some of the most progressive places, because the members are forced to know each other and by extension are forced to get along. I believe Marfa is a progressive small town. Recently, Marfa Independent School District installed a gender-neutral restroom in the high school for its one transgender student, who was also profiled in the paper.[29] In 2011, locals created Occupy Marfa to echo the larger movement happening in Lower Manhattan,[30] and most recently, a small but proud group of protesters organized a "solidarity march" to mirror the Women's March in Washington, one day after President Trump's inauguration.[31] As one local described to me, "People know about each other's business, but I don't think that people care, or it really matters to people. I don't get the sense that Marfa is a particularly judgy place. I think you can really be yourself and not worry about that."

Despite the varying priorities and interests of its Hispanic, ranching, and arts-focused residents, Marfa remains a pleasant and friendly town that continues to attract visitors and transplants. Its cultural programming, border politics, and environmental challenges have continued to attract steady media attention, which further serves to focus interest and curiosity from outsiders. Marfa may be remote, but it is not isolated.

Perhaps, though, it is Sean Wilsey who put it best regarding the changes occurring in Marfa: "Where once so little seemed likely to happen that I'd walk around open to everything, now, with the town in a constant state of *happeningness*, I felt a need to shut it all out."[32]

Marfans will continue to have *their* Marfa, while visitors will continue to experience a separate, focused Marfa. Both experiences are valid, just different. Robert Irwin's finished piece will bring a wealth of new media attention and subsequent tourists, and many of those who continue to hear about Marfa, for whatever the reason, will make the journey to find out for themselves what this place is about.

As another local noted, "You can't preserve Marfa as a dollhouse," but the participation of Marfa's community members will be essential in sustaining the qualities that have always drawn its residents and visitors—the land and the light.

My first visit to Marfa brought me through El Paso, via US Airways, and so that was my initial entrance to the landscape. Since then, I've come to Marfa from Austin, a six-hour drive. It's a different feeling to come to Marfa this way, a long drive that is also surprisingly easy to make. There are many small towns to pass through along the way—Johnson City, Stonewall, Harper, Junction—and my goal has always been Marfa, so I've invested few minutes in these other places. There is, in reality, so much to see.

When I leave Marfa to head back to Austin, I'm within range of Marfa Public Radio for about an hour and a half; after that, I'll need to scan for something new.

ACKNOWLEDGMENTS

Thanks to my teachers Paul Adams, Steve Hoelscher, Randy Lewis, Leo Zonn, and the late Karl Butzer for their guidance and mentorship throughout my tenure at UT Austin, where this book began.

Thanks to the many people in Marfa who shared their stories and welcomed me into their community.

Thanks to my editor, Emily Ethridge, who cleaned up and rearranged many sentences, and to my editor at UT Press, Robert Devens, for his support and enthusiasm.

NOTES

CHAPTER 1. INTRODUCTION

1. Although Far West Texas is an identifiable region, I use the term "West Texas" in this book. Both terms are acceptable and are often used interchangeably. Unsurprisingly, Far West Texas defines a narrower region than West Texas.

2. Annual mean precipitation for Marfa is 15.79" and for Presidio County is 10.76." Source: Office of the Texas State Climatologist, Texas A&M University.

3. Lucy Miller Jacobson and Mildred Bloys Nored, *Jeff Davis County, Texas* (Fort Davis, TX: Fort Davis Historical Society, 1993).

4. Michael Graczyk, "Fashion Meets West Texas in Unlikely Art Project," *Plainview Daily*, February 10, 2006.

5. Michael Graczyk, "Vandals Target Quirky Artsy West Texas Prada Marfa," *Washington Times*, March 25, 2011.

6. Graczyk, "Fashion Meets West Texas."

7. John Daniel Garcia, "Stealth Artist May Be Behind Latest Prada Marfa Vandalism," *Big Bend Sentinel* (Marfa, TX), March 10, 2014.

8. Sarah M. Vasquez, "Target Marathon, Another Roadside Attraction," *Big Bend Sentinel* (Marfa, TX), January 21, 2016.

9. Graczyk, "Vandals Target Quirky Artsy West Texas Prada Marfa."

10. "Service Saturday for Donald Judd," *Big Bend Sentinel* (Marfa, TX), February 17, 1994.

11. See Denis Cosgrove and Stephen Daniels, eds., *The Iconography of Landscape: Essays on the Symbolic Representation, Design and Use of Past Environments* (Cambridge: Cambridge University Press, 1988); Denis E. Cosgrove, *Social Formation and Symbolic Landscape* (Madison: University of Wisconsin Press, 1998); John Brinckerhoff Jackson, *Discovering the Vernacular Landscape* (New Haven, CT: Yale University Press, 1984); Yi-Fu Tuan, *Space and Place: The Perspective of Experience* (Minneapolis: University of Minnesota Press, 1977); Yi-Fu Tuan, *Topophilia: A Study of Environmental Perceptions, Attitudes, and Values* (New York: Columbia University Press, 1990).

12. Susan Spano and Aviva Shen, "The 20 Best Small Towns in America of 2012," *Smithsonian*, May 2012; and Ondine Cohane, "52 Places to Go in 2016," *New York Times*, January 6, 2016; Web, April 23, 2016, http:// www.nytimes.com/interactive/2016/01/07/travel/places-to-visit .html?place=grandrapids.

13. For example, *Big Art in a One Horse Town*, directed by Ian MacMillan, BBC, 1995, DVD; *Marfa: The Land and the Light*, directed by Joseph Cashiola, KLRU: Arts in Context, 2011; Morley Safer, writer, "Marfa, Texas: The Capital of Quirkiness," on *60 Minutes*, CBS, April 14, 2013.

14. Julia Lawlor, "The Great Marfa . . . Land Boom," *New York Times*, April 29, 2005; Arthur Lubow, "The Art Land," *New York Times*, March 20, 2005; Michael Hall, "'The Buzz About Marfa Is Just Crazy,'" *Texas Monthly*, September 2004, 136–142; B. Strickland, "Art Oasis," *Travel and Leisure*, September 2005, 86ff.; Sean Wilsey and Daphne Beal, "Lone Star Bohemia," *Vanity Fair*, July 2012; Penelope Green, "A Moth to Marfa's Flame," *New York Times*, February 29, 2012.

15. Pierre Bourdieu, *The Field of Cultural Production* (New York: Columbia University Press, 1993).

16. "Buy a First Edition in Archer City," from "The Bucket List," *Texas Monthly*, March 2010, 180, accessed July 2, 2013, http://www.texasmonthly.com /story/bucket-list/page/0/8; Edie Adelstein, "Green Mountain Falls, the Next Marfa?," *Colorado Springs Independent*, November 1, 2012; Jonathan Thompson, "Forgiving Winslow, Arizona—Not Just Another Marfa," *High Country News*, September 9, 2013; Erin Shaw Street, "Is Elkmont, Alabama the Next Marfa?," *The Daily South*, June 26, 2014.

17. See E. C. Relph, *Place and Placelessness* (London: Pion, 1976); John Urry and Jonas Larsen, *The Tourist Gaze* (London: Sage Publications, 2002); Rebecca Maria Torres and Janet D. Momsen, "Gringolandia: The Construction of a New Tourist Space in Mexico," *Annals of the Association of American Geographers* 95, no. 2 (2005): 314–335.

18. John K. Wright, "Terrae Incognitae: The Place of the Imagination in Geography," *Annals of the Association of American Geographers* 37, no. 1 (1947): 1–15.

19. Ibid., 2.

20. Ibid., 5.

21. See Josh T. Franco, "Marfa, Marfa: Minimalism, Rasquachismo, and Questioning 'Decolonial Aesthetics' in Far West Texas" (PhD diss., Binghamton University, 2016); Michael Seman, "No Country for Old Developers: The Strange Tale of an Arts Boom, Bohemians, and 'Marfalafel' in the High Desert of Marfa, Texas," *Applied Research in Economic Development* 5, no. 3 (2008): 25–31; Martha Schnee, "Going West: An Interdisciplinary Study of Marfa, Texas" (Honors thesis, Bates College, 2015).

CHAPTER 2. THE HISTORY OF MARFA

1. Anne Kelly Knowles, *Placing History: How Maps, Spatial Data, and GIS Are Changing Historical Scholarship* (Redlands, CA: Esri Press, 2008), 11.

2. Jefferson Morgenthaler, *The River Has Never Divided Us: A Border History of La Junta de los Rios* (Austin: University of Texas Press, 2004).

3. Ibid.

4. Susan J. Tweit, *Barren, Wild, and Worthless: Living in the Chihuahuan Desert* (Albuquerque: University of New Mexico Press, 1995), 9.

5. Morgenthaler, *The River Has Never Divided Us*, 23.

6. Source: US Census Bureau, 2010.

7. For a detailed discussion of the treaty, see Morgenthaler, *The River Has Never Divided Us*.

8. US Department of the Interior, *Report on the United States and Mexican Boundary Survey: Made under the Direction of the Secretary of the Interior by William H. Emory, Major First Cavalry, and United States Commissioner*, Rep. Vol., 3 vols. bound in 2 (Washington, DC: C. Wendell, Printer, 1857–1859). The survey had been a joint effort between the countries on both sides of the river. As the area to survey was large, this accounts for why it took this long to complete following the Mexican-American War.

9. Michael Hall, "The Truth Is Out There," *Texas Monthly*, June 2006.

10. Ibid.

11. Interview with Georgie Lee Kahl, from an unpublished memoir by her husband, Fritz Kahl.

12. Chris Riemenschneider, "Of Gaseous Jack Rabbits, Dead Apache Chiefs and a Phenomenon Cool enough for James Dean, The Marfa Mystery Lights," *Austin American-Statesman*, October 28, 1999.

13. Judith Brueske, *The Marfa Lights*, 2nd rev. ed. (Alpine, TX: Ocotillo Enterprises, 1988); James Bunnell, *Night Orbs: An Exploration into Unknown Luminous Phenomena* (Cedar Creek, TX: Lacey Pub., 2003).

14. "Legend: Marfa Lights," on *Unsolved Mysteries*, October 25, 1989.

15. Riemenschneider, "Of Gaseous Jack Rabbits . . ."

16. Bunnell, *Night Orbs*; Weston Sedgwick, "In Search of Spring Break and Marfa Lights," *The Pantagraph* (Bloomington, IL), April 13, 1999.

17. John Burnett, writer, "Cause of 'Marfa Lights' Either UFOs or Car Headlights," on NPR, April 1, 1994.

18. Paul Simons, "Mystery Lights That Hang over Marfa," *Times* (London), November 17, 2005.

19. Ibid.

20. Megan Lea Buck, "Marfa Lights Inspire Conspiracy Novel," Associated Press, August 10, 2009.

21. Cecilia Thompson, *History of Marfa and Presidio County, Texas, 1535–1946* (Austin, TX: Nortex, 1985).

22. Ibid., 182.

23. Ibid.

24. Source: US Census Bureau, 1900.

25. *Big Bend Sentinel* (Marfa, TX), November 6, 1930.

26. In other parts of West Texas (Midland, Odessa, and other areas outside of the Chihuahuan Desert), the business of oil continues. See James Osborne, "After Decades of Busts and Booms, Oil Fields around Midland and Odessa Are . . . ," *Dallas Morning News*, November 2, 2013, accessed November 6, 2013, http://res.dallasnews.com/interactives/2013_November/oilboom.

27. As quoted in Thompson, *History of Marfa and Presidio County*.

28. Ibid.

29. I will not attempt to summarize the Mexican Revolution but instead note that its history is as complex and controversial as any war or conflict. Myriad books have been written on the subject, including but not limited to Frank McLynn, *Villa and Zapata: A History of the Mexican Revolution* (New York: Carroll and Graf, 2001); Stuart Easterling, *The Mexican Revolution: A Short History, 1910–1920* (Chicago, IL: Haymarket, 2012); Mark Wasserman, *The Mexican Revolution: A Brief History with Documents* (Boston: Bedford/St. Martins, 2012); Anita Brenner and George Ross Leighton, *The Wind That Swept Mexico: The History of the Mexican Revolution, 1910–1942* (Austin: University of Texas Press, 1971); Mariano Azuela, *The Underdogs: A Novel of the Mexican Revolution* ([New York]: New American Library, 1963).

30. See Gerald G. Raun, "Seventeen Days in November: The Lynching of Antonio Rodriguez and American-Mexican Relations, November 3–19,

1910," *The Journal of Big Bend Studies* 7 (1995); Marianne Bachman Kerr, "Corridos: Reflections in Acculturation along the Border," *The Journal of Big Bend Studies* 7 (1995), 203–216; Paul Wright, "A Tumultuous Decade: Changes in the Mexican-Origin Population of the Big Bend, 1910–1920." *The Journal of Big Bend Studies* 10 (1998).

31. A 2016 dissertation on Marfa ("Marfa, Marfa: Minimalism, Rasquachismo, and Questioning 'Decolonial Aesthetics' in Far West Texas") by Josh T. Franco (PhD, Art History, Binghamton University) specifically explores the discrepancies between white and Hispanic identities, involving but not limited to the type of pilgrimages undertaken by visitors to Marfa.

32. Thompson, *History of Marfa and Presidio County*.

33. Ibid.

34. Fort D. A. Russell in Wyoming was renamed to honor the late Senator of Wyoming Francis E. Warren, so the name Russell was transferred to Camp Marfa.

35. Federal subsidies are not my area of expertise, but throughout history and especially tied to times of war, they play an integral part in the economic makeup and sustainability of various industries. A few notes on wool and mohair can be found in Charles D. Hyson, "Maladjustments in the Wool Industry and Need for New Policy," *Journal of Farm Economics* 29, no. 2 (1947): 425–456; Glen D. Whipple and Dale J. Menkhaus, "Supply Response in the U.S. Sheep Industry," *American Journal of Agricultural Economics* 71, no. 1 (1989): 126–135; Jerry J. Jasinowski, "The Great Fiscal Unknown—Subsidies," *The American Journal of Economics and Sociology* 32, no. 1 (1973): 1–16.

36. Source: https://www.cbp.gov/border-security/along-us-borders/border-patrol-sectors/big-bend-sector-texas.

37. Interview with William Brooks, US Customs and Border Protection, Marfa, 2011.

38. Dan McNichol, *The Roads That Built America: The Incredible Story of the U.S. Interstate System* (New York: Sterling, 2006), and Tom Lewis, *Divided Highways: Building the Interstate Highways, Transforming American Life* (New York: Viking, 1997).

39. See Jack W. Burgess, PE, *Technical Report on Shafter Feasibility Study: Presidio County, Texas, USA*, technical paper (Vancouver, BC: Aurcana Corporation, 2011); Alberto Tomas Halpern, "Shafter Silver Now Being Mined," *Big Bend Sentinel* (Marfa, TX), June 7, 2012; Michael Graczyk, "Texas Silver Mine Gets New Life after 1942 Closure," Associated Press, March 19, 2011.

40. Sterry Butcher, "Fort Davis Couple Buys Historic El Paisano Hotel," *Big Bend Sentinel* (Marfa, TX), March 8, 2001.

41. The other three sites are the Presidio County Courthouse, Building 98 at Fort D. A. Russell, and the greater Fort D. A. Russell historic district.

42. As evidenced by *Big Bend Sentinel* articles during this period.

43. Arnold P. Krammer, "When the 'Afrika Korps' Came to Texas," *Southwestern Historical Quarterly* 80, no. 3 (1977): 247–282.

44. Lonn Taylor, "Fort D. A. Russell, Marfa," lecture, The Chinati Foundation, Marfa, Texas, May 1, 2011.

45. Allen Anthony, *Little Airlines in the Big Bend* (Fort Davis, TX: River Microstudies, 1999).

46. As told to me by the local pilot and Marfa resident Burt Compton.

47. For more information, see http://archinect.com/people/project/5290 3780/maaf/54037381.

48. Sterry Butcher, "Motorcar Raceway Speeding toward Marfa Army Airfield?," *Big Bend Sentinel* (Marfa, TX), February 10, 2011.

49. The 1950s drought was as bad as that of the 1930s, or the Dust Bowl years, and although culturally the Dust Bowl is most often thought of as being contained in the Great Plains, its effects were seen all over the United States, including Far West Texas. In fact, one of the Farm Security Administration (FSA) photographers, Russell Lee, photographed the Walking X Ranch near Marfa in 1939. See Kurt Schwabe, Jose Albiac-Murillo, Jeffrey D. Connor, Rashid M. Hassan, and Liliana Meza González, eds., *Drought in Arid and Semi-Arid Regions: A Multi-disciplinary and Cross-country Perspective* (Dordrecht, Netherlands: Springer, 2013); Michael H. Glantz, *Drought Follows the Plow: Cultivating Marginal Areas* (Cambridge: Cambridge University Press, 1994).

50. Michael Graczyk, "50 Years Later, Movie Classic a Touchstone for West Texas Town," *Plainview Daily Herald*, July 1, 2005, http://www.myplain view.com/news/article/Fifty-years-later-Giant-remains-movie-classic -8541771.php.

51. Editorial, "Negative Light Creating Quite a Gray Area," *Austin American-Statesman*, May 22, 2009.

52. Thadis W. Box, "Range Deterioration in West Texas," *Southwestern Historical Quarterly* 71, no. 1 (1967): 37–45.

53. Luke Brite, "Reflections," quoted in Thompson, *History of Marfa and Presidio County*.

54. "2015 Land Report 100," *The Land Report*, accessed July 10, 2016, http://www.landreport.com/americas-100-largest-landowners/.

55. The manager, Jim White III, is a fourth-generation grandson.

56. See http://dixonwater.org/about-us.

57. M. Paulsen, "Fatal Error: The Pentagon's War on Drugs Takes a Toll on the Innocent," *Austin Chronicle*, December 25, 1998.

58. S. Gwynne, "Border Skirmish," *Time*, August 25, 1997, 40.

59. Sterry Butcher, "After 5 Years, Redford Teen's Killing Still Troubles Participants in Case," *Big Bend Sentinel*, May 16, 2002, 1, 7.

60. Douglas Kent Hall, *The Border: Life on the Line* (New York: Abbeville Press, 1988).

61. Quoting US Border Patrol Agent Mike Harrison, in Hall, *The Border*.

62. For example, in 1991, 8,957 illegals were captured; in 1992 that rose to 11,690; and in 1993 it rose again, to 15,920.

63. Editorial, "Twisting the Truth on the Mexican Border," *Washington Post*, May 14, 2011.

64. The Southwest Sector is composed of Big Bend (Marfa), Del Rio, El Centro, El Paso, Laredo, Rio Grande Valley (McAllen), San Diego, Tucson, Yuma, and, as of FY 2010, the Special Operations Group. For comparison, the Coastal Border Sectors increased from 183 to 224, and the Northern Border Sectors increased from 310 to 2,206 in the same time period.

65. The 2010 census for Marfa shows 69 percent Hispanic; the 2000 census shows 70 percent Hispanic; the 1990 census shows 68 percent Hispanic. Information in previous years does not show Hispanic origin; however, in 1980, 77 percent of the population of the entire Presidio County was Hispanic. Previous census data did not record demographic data; however, an interview with the former principal and then superintendent of the Marfa Independent School District from 1964 to 1992 revealed that in 1965, the school demographics were roughly 70 percent Hispanic, which suggests a similar overall demographic to Marfa. Another native said that during her high school years in the 1950s, classes were largely Hispanic.

66. Tony Cano, *The Other Side of the Tracks* (Canutillo, TX: Reata Press; Kearney, NE: Morris Publishing, 2001).

67. Although there was a special school supplement to the January 21 edition of the *Big Bend Sentinel*, the writing focused on the dedication of the new Marfa Elementary School as well as a profile of Jesse Blackwell, the teacher for whom the Blackwell School was renamed in 1942. There was no critical discussion of what it meant at the time to integrate two previously segregated schools into one.

68. From interviews with former students, but also see Mary Walling Blackburn, "A Politics of Tears: The Museum of Useless Efforts, Marfa, TX," *Afterall*, May 11, 2008, accessed December 2, 2013.

69. Francesca Mari, "The Economics of Marfa," *The Art Newspaper*, 251, November 2013; the quote is from a comment that follows the article; see http://old.theartnewspaper.com/articles/The-economics-of-Marfa/30955.

70. In 2016, city council members include Manuel V. Baeza, Genevieve Bassham, Mark Scott, and Peter Stanley.

71. From an interview with the Marfa native Joe Cabezuela. See Louise S. O'Connor and Cecilia Thompson, *Marfa and Presidio County, Texas*, Vol. 2 (N.p.: Xlibris, 2014).

72. Safer, "Marfa, Texas."

73. Thomas Wilson, "Dostoyevsky and the Big Bend," *The Journal of Big Bend Studies* 13 (2001): 121–144.

74. See H. Bailey Carroll, "Texas Collection," *Southwestern Historical Quarterly* 48, no. 2 (1944): 276–303, which names *Michael Strogoff* as the source. See Richard West, *The Last Frontier*, Texas Monthly, November 1977, which names the Russian novella *Marfa Posadnitsa* as the source.

75. Wilson, "Dostoyevsky and the Big Bend."

76. As told to me by Cecilia Thompson.

77. Wilson, "Dostoyevsky and the Big Bend."

78. Ibid.

79. *Daily News* (Galveston), December 17, 1882, accessed July 2, 2013, http://galveston.newspaperarchive.com.

80. Thompson, *History of Marfa and Presidio County*.

81. Mary Bones, "The Lost Colony: Texas Regionalist Paintings," *Cenizo Journal* (Alpine, TX), Winter 2011.

82. Interview with Cecilia Thompson.

83. And I haven't even touched upon Hispanic art, which is my own fault as a nonexpert. See Josh T. Franco's 2016 dissertation, which expands on Hispanic culture and art in West Texas.

84. *Big Bend Sentinel*, November 6, 1930.

CHAPTER 3. ENCOUNTERING THE LANDSCAPE OF MARFA

1. Carl Sauer, "The Morphology of Landscape," in John Leighly, ed., *Land and Life: A Selection from the Writings of Carl Ortwin Sauer* (Berkeley: University of California, 1963); Cosgrove and Daniels, *The Iconography of Landscape*.

2. Donald Meinig, *The Interpretation of Ordinary Landscapes: Geographical Essays* (New York: Oxford University Press, 1979), 1.

3. Tuan, *Topophilia*.

4. Cosgrove, *Social Formation and Symbolic Landscape*.

5. Cosgrove and Daniels. *The Iconography of Landscape*.

6. W. J. T. Mitchell, *Landscape and Power* (Chicago: University of Chicago, 1994).

7. Gary L. Gaile and Cort J. Willmott, eds., *Geography in America at the Dawn of the 21st Century* (Oxford: Oxford University Press, 2003).

8. Rachel B. Doyle, "The Desert Beckons in a Designer's Minimalist Marfa Abode," *Curbed*, April 2, 2015; Misty Keasler and Amanda Dameron,

"This Former Dance Hall Gets an Encore and Becomes a Designer's House," *Dwell*, August 28, 2016.

9. D. H. Shurbet and C. C. Reeves, "The Fill in Marfa Basin, Texas," *AAPG Bulletin* 61 (1977): 612–615.

10. Tuan, *Space and Place*.

11. Some examples of these events are the following: Marfa Film Festival, CineMarfa Film Festival, Marfa Dialogues, Trans-Pecos Music Festival, MARFArchitecture + Design Symposium.

12. Relph, *Place and Placelessness*.

13. Marc Augé, *Non-places: Introduction to an Anthropology of Supermodernity* (London: Verso, 1995, 2009).

14. Victor W. Turner and Edith L. B. Turner, *Image and Pilgrimage in Christian Culture: Anthropological Perspectives* (New York: Columbia University Press, 1978), 241, quoted in Nick Couldry, "Pilgrimage in Mediaspace: Continuities and Transformations," *Etnofoor* 20, no. 1 (2007): 63–73.

15. Michael Kimmelman, "The Art of the Pilgrimage," in *The Accidental Masterpiece: On the Art of Life and Vice Versa* (New York: Penguin, 2005), 186.

16. Jeanne Claire van Ryzin, "A Little Take on Marfa's Culture Clash," *Austin American-Statesman*, October 26, 2011.

17. Larry McMurtry, *Walter Benjamin at the Dairy Queen: Reflections at Sixty and Beyond* (New York: Simon and Schuster, 1999).

18. According to the 2013 US Census.

19. Ardis Cameron, "When Strangers Bring Cameras: The Poetics and Politics of Othered Places," *American Quarterly* 54, no. 3 (2002): 411.

20. Donald Meinig, "Geography as an Art," *Transaction of the Institute of British Geographers* 8, no. 3 (1983): 314–328; quote from p. 325.

21. Le Corbusier, with an introduction by Jean-Louis Cohen and translated by John Goodman, *Toward an Architecture* (Los Angeles, CA: Getty Research Institute, 2007).

22. Jake Silverstein, "Sterry Butcher, Small-Town Newspaper Reporter," *Texas Monthly*, August 2007.

CHAPTER 4. DONALD JUDD IN MARFA

1. Sterry Butcher, "Striving for Balance, Marfa Comes of Age," *Big Bend Sentinel* (Marfa, TX), October 9, 2003.

2. Donald Judd, *Complete Writings, 1959–1975: Gallery Reviews, Book Reviews, Articles, Letters to the Editor, Reports, Statements, Complaints* (Halifax, N.S.: Press of the Nova Scotia College of Art and Design, 1975), 15.

3. Donald Judd, "Specific Objects," *Arts Yearbook* 8 (1965): 74–82.

4. In the published essay, one of Judd's pieces is included as an illustration, but he notes that "the editor, not I, included the photograph of my work." The essay includes seventeen photographs, and Judd references about forty-five artists.

5. Phrases from "Specific Objects."

6. See Smith's written lecture in Marianne Stockebrand, *The Writings of Donald Judd: A Symposium Hosted by the Chinati Foundation, Marfa, Texas, May 3–4, 2008* (Marfa, TX: Chinati Foundation, 2009), 73.

7. See Clement Greenberg, *Art and Culture: Critical Essays* (Boston: Beacon, 1989); Michael Fried, *Art and Objecthood: Essays and Reviews* (Chicago: University of Chicago, 1998).

8. Donald Judd, "Complaints, Part I," *Studio International* (April 1969), 198; this essay appears in Judd, *Complete Writings, 1959–1975*.

9. Donald Judd, Flavin Judd, and Caitlin Murray, "A Long Discussion Not about Masterpieces but Why There Are So Few of Them: Part II (1984)," in *Donald Judd: Writings* (New York: Judd Foundation, 2016), 382.

10. Marianne Stockebrand, Donald Judd, and Rudi Fuchs, *Chinati: The Vision of Donald Judd* (Marfa, TX: Chinati Foundation, 2010).

11. Donald Judd, Flavin Judd, and Caitlin Murray, "On Installation (1982)," in *Donald Judd: Writings* (New York: Judd Foundation, 2016), 309.

12. See Donald Judd, "Complaints, Part II," *Arts Magazine* (June 1973), for a detailed review of damages. He describes the mishandling of his work by art handlers, the carelessness of museum staff and guards, and the failure of catalogues to accurately reflect the details of each work.

13. Judd, *Complete Writings*.

14. Donald Judd, "In Defense of My Work," in *Chinati*.

15. Donald Judd, "Marfa, Texas," in *Chinati*.

16. Ibid.

17. Ibid.

18. Royce Flying Field, located about where the present-day golf course is.

19. Ibid.

20. Krista Thornsburg Ackerman, *Big Bend Sentinel*, June 17, 1999.

21. See www.diaart.org and Melissa Susan Gaido Allen, "From the Dia to the Chinati Foundation: Donald Judd in Marfa, Texas, 1979–1994" (master's thesis, Rice University, 1995).

22. As quoted in Stockebrand, Judd, and Fuchs, *Chinati*, 32.

23. Bob Colacello, "Remains of the Dia," *Vanity Fair*, April 30, 2008.

24. See Grace Glueck, "The De Menil Family: The Medici of Modern Art," *New York Times*, May 18, 1986; Josef Helfenstein and Laureen Schipsi, eds., *Art and Activism: Projects of John and Dominique de Menil* (Houston: Menil Collection, 2010); Marie-Alain Couturier, with texts selected

by Dominique de Menil and Pie Duployé, translated by Granger Ryan, *Sacred Art* (Austin: University of Texas Press, 1989); Ken Auletta, *The Art of Corporate Success: The Story of Schlumberger* (New York: Putnam, 1984); Anne Gruner Schlumberger, *The Schlumberger Adventure: Two Brothers Who Pioneered in Petroleum Technology* (New York: Arco, 1982); Colacello, "Remains of the Dia."

25. Stockebrand, Judd, and Fuchs, *Chinati.*
26. Allen, "From the Dia to the Chinati Foundation."
27. Ibid.
28. Ibid. For a detailed description of events, see Allen, "From the Dia to the Chinati Foundation."
29. Stockebrand, Judd, and Fuchs, *Chinati.*
30. Marianne Stockebrand, Rob Weiner, and Jeffrey Kopie.
31. While the Chinati Foundation was established during Judd's lifetime, the Judd Foundation was created after many years of organizing his estate after his death. See Sterry Butcher, "Chinati Foundation Judd's Grand Vision," *Big Bend Sentinel* (Marfa, TX), February 17, 1994; Sterry Butcher, "Life after Judd," *Big Bend Sentinel* (Marfa, TX), June 30, 1994; Rosario Salgado Halpern, "Foundation at Crossroads," *Big Bend Sentinel* (Marfa, TX), June 30, 1994; "Chinati Art Foundation Evolving into Judd's Vision," *Big Bend Sentinel* (Marfa, TX), March 21, 1996.
32. Judd was also a designer of furniture, and his pieces are still produced by the Judd Foundation.
33. The criticism, as I understand it and as told to me throughout various interviews, is that the outside world focuses on the artiness of Marfa, despite the fact that not all residents of Marfa have anything to do with the art.
34. Phil Cousineau, *Art of Pilgrimage: The Seeker's Guide to Making Travel Sacred* (Berkeley, CA: Conari, 2012); Jessica Dawson, "Exploring Art's Remote Possibilities," *Washington Post*, July 15, 2001.
35. Chinati tours are free to residents of Presidio, Jeff Davis, and Brewster Counties. The full tour is $25 and $10 for students. The selections tour is $20 and $10 for students. The newly available self-guided tour of the artillery sheds is $10 and $5 for students. The outdoor concrete works are freely accessible during museum hours.
36. Phone interview with Jenny Moore, Marfa, 2017.
37. Stockebrand, Judd, and Fuchs, *Chinati.*
38. Ibid.
39. See *Art & Place: Site-Specific Art of the Americas* (London: Phaidon, 2013); Amy Dempsey, *Destination Art* (Berkeley: University of California Press, 2006); Miwon Kwon, *One Place after Another: Site-Specific Art and Locational Identity* (Cambridge, MA: MIT Press, 2002).

40. Serra, quoted in Kwon, *One Place after Another*, 12.

41. Stockebrand, Judd, and Fuchs, *Chinati*.

42. "Nevertheless, in reworking the old buildings, I've turned them into architecture." See his essay "The Chinati Foundation/La Fundación Chinati" from 1987, printed in Stockebrand, Judd, and Fuchs, *Chinati*, 281.

43. Allen, "From the Dia to the Chinati Foundation."

44. Interview with Valerie Arber, Marfa, 2012; she had led the tour where this remark was made.

45. Interview with James Rodewald, Marfa, 2011.

46. For more bibliographic information, see Michael Govan and Tiffany Bell, *Dan Flavin: The Complete Lights, 1961–1996* (New York: Dia Art Foundation in association with Yale University Press, 2004); Dan Flavin and Tiffany Bell, *Light in Architecture and Art: The Work of Dan Flavin* (Marfa, TX: Chinati Foundation, 2002); Roberta Smith, "Dan Flavin, 63, Sculptor of Fluorescent Light, Dies," *New York Times*, December 4, 1996.

47. Stockebrand, Judd, and Fuchs, *Chinati*.

48. Steve Delahoyde, "Thomas Kellein Named New Director of Donald Judd's Chinati Foundation," *Media Bistro*, August 10, 2010.

49. Michael Kimmelman, "The Last Great Art of the 20th Century," *New York Times*, February 4, 2001.

50. For more bibliographic information, see Randy Kennedy, "John Chamberlain, Who Wrested Rough Magic from Scrap Metal, Dies at 84," *New York Times*, December 21, 2011; John Chamberlain and William C. Agee, *It's All in the Fit: The Work of John Chamberlain: A Symposium Hosted by the Chinati Foundation, Marfa, Texas, April 22–23, 2006* (Marfa, TX: Chinati Foundation, 2009).

51. Robert Irwin and Lawrence Weschler, *Being and Circumstance: Notes toward a Conditional Art* (Larkspur Landing, CA: Lapis in conjunction with the Pace Gallery and the San Francisco Museum of Modern Art, 1985).

52. See https://chinati.org/programs/chinati-announces-team-for-master-plan-grant-from-andrew-w-mellon-foundation.

53. For more on this controversy, see "Chinati Announces Major New Work by Robert Irwin," *Big Bend Sentinel* (Marfa, TX), October 9, 2014; "Chinati Hosts Irwin Installation Meeting," *Big Bend Sentinel* (Marfa, TX), November 26, 2014; Mark Lamster, "A Question of Vision in Marfa," *The Dallas Morning News*, July 2, 2015, http://interactives.dallasnews.com/2015/marfa/; Sarah M. Vasquez, "With Controversy behind Them, Irwin Project Under Way," *Big Bend Sentinel* (Marfa, TX), October 8, 2015.

54. John Daniel Garcia, "Fort D. A. Russell Home Spared the Wrecking Ball," *Big Bend Sentinel* (Marfa, TX), October 16, 2014.

55. Source: http://www.juddfoundation.org.

56. So named for the former owners.
57. The Studios tour is $30 and $15 for students, and the Block tour is $20 and $10 for students.
58. This is how my tour guide referred to the pool.
59. Patrick Lynch, "Donald Judd's Architectural Fury," *Architect's Journal*, November 24, 2008, Web, accessed July 2, 2013, https://www.architects journal.co.uk/donald-judds-architectural-fury/1931822.article.
60. Judd was also a prolific furniture designer. Although he made a distinction between his art and his furniture, there is a clear aesthetic and philosophical connection between the two.
61. The Lannan Foundation is a writer-in-residence program in Marfa that is discussed in later sections.
62. Peter Reading, *Marfan* (Newcastle upon Tyne, UK: Bloodaxe, 2000).
63. Ibid.
64. This would have been between 1980 and 1984, though an exact date is unknown.
65. See Tony McIntyre, "Culture: The Other End of Infinity," *Building Design* (October 2007): 22. McIntyre wrote that it was ironic, but it is instead part of the larger story of Marfa, of its rebirth as a place of art and culture instead of becoming a ghost town. I've already described how the military's abandonment of Fort D. A. Russell and the Marfa Army Airfield, as well as the drought of the 1950s, caused an exodus of residents from Marfa. The infrastructure of space, in the form of military and historic buildings, is what Judd encountered on his early trips to Marfa in the 1970s. The space was there, unused, and in repurposing the buildings, he made it place.
66. Paul DiMaggio and Michael Useem, "Social Class and Arts Consumption: The Origins and Consequences of Class Differences in Exposure to the Arts in America," *Theory and Society* 5 (1978): 141–161.
67. Ibid., 144.
68. Anna Chave, "Minimalism and the Rhetoric of Power," *Arts Magazine* 64, no. 5 (January 1990): 44–63; quote from p. 117.
69. Greenberg, quoted in Chave, "Minimalism and the Rhetoric of Power," 118.
70. Judd, *Complete Writings*.
71. In *Specific Objects*, Judd makes note of contemporary artists who he felt were pushing the boundaries of painting, for instance, Frank Stella, Larry Bell, and Lee Bontecou. Stella's shapely canvases defied the tradition of rectangular form in painting; Bell's use of industrial glass and Plexiglas challenged traditional notions of sculpture; and Bontecou's sculpture nearly reads as 3-D painting, a monochromatic sculpture within a rectangular, painting-like format.

72. Judd did not agree with the term "minimalism" and instead chose to see himself as an empiricist. However, he is commonly referred to as a minimalist artist in the context of modern art history.

73. Judd, *Complete Writings*, 184.

74. Cosgrove, *Social Formation and Symbolic Landscape*.

75. Henri Lefebvre, *The Production of Space* (Oxford, UK: Blackwell, 1992).

76. Gaston Bachelard and Maria Jolas, *The Poetics of Space* (Boston: Beacon, 1994).

77. Jean Lescure, quoted in ibid., xxxiii.

78. Donald Judd, Flavin Judd, and Caitlin Murray, "Russian Art in Regard to Myself (1981)," in *Donald Judd: Writings*, 298.

79. Many of the books in his library remain unopened or have unbroken spines, signifying his intention of creating a reference library or catalogue of information regardless of whether or not he had any intention of reading them, and when considered with the number of spaces Judd occupied in Marfa and the number of objects contained within them, it leads me to believe that Judd was actually quite a hoarder.

80. Joe Nick Patoski, "What Would Donald Judd Do?," July 2001, http://www.joenickp.com/texas/donaldjudd.html.

81. Judd, "Marfa, Texas," in *Chinati*.

82. Judd, *Complete Writings*.

83. Judd, "Arena," in *Chinati*.

84. Judd, "Marfa, Texas," in *Chinati*.

85. Donald Judd, Flavin Judd, and Caitlin Murray, *Donald Judd: Writings*, 11.

CHAPTER 5. MARFA AFTER JUDD

1. Roberta Smith, "The World according to Judd," *New York Times*, February 26, 1995.

2. Neda Ulaby, "Marfa, Texas: An Unlikely Art Oasis in a Desert Town," NPR, August 2, 2012.

3. Sterry Butcher, "Chinati Foundation Sees Rise in Visitors by Educators, Classes," *Big Bend Sentinel* (Marfa, TX), March 23, 2000.

4. Source: Caitlin Murray of the Judd Foundation.

5. "Exhibition and Museum Attendance Figures 2010," *Art Newspaper* (London), April 2011.

6. Michael Barnes, "West to Marfa for New Year's Eve," January 4, 2012, http://www.austin360.com/news/entertainment/arts-theater/west-to-marfa-for-new-years-eve-1/nRjSc.

7. Interview with Tim Crowley, Marfa, 2012.

8. Tim and Lynn divorced in 2008, so any future use of Tim's name only is deliberate.

9. Various sources say he employed between twenty and sixty-three people throughout the years.

10. As told to me by the locals Robert and Valerie Arber.

11. This was unfortunately short-lived, as the coffee and wine bar has since been removed.

12. The John Wesley gallery opened in 2004, and the Robert Irwin exhibit opened in 2016.

13. Sterry Butcher, "Flavin Installation Completes Judd's Vision for Chinati," *Big Bend Sentinel* (Marfa, TX), October 5, 2000.

14. Rosario Salgado Halpern, "Artisans Acquiring Marfa Properties," *Big Bend Sentinel* (Marfa, TX), July 3, 1997.

15. Interview with Charles Mary Kubricht, 2011.

16. A tangent here but fascinating in its own right. See Roy R. Behrens, *Ship Shape, a Dazzle Camouflage Sourcebook: An Anthology of Writings about Ship Camouflage during World War One* (Dysart, IA: Bobolink Books, 2012).

17. For a complete list of past residents, see http://chinati.org/programs /artists-in-residence.

18. Source: http://www.fieldworkmarfa.org/node/2.

19. Source: http://www.lannan.org/about.

20. Sterry Butcher, "Lannan Foundation Program Grows with House Purchases," *Big Bend Sentinel* (Marfa, TX), May 3, 2001.

21. Sterry Butcher, "Lannan Foundation Purchases Sixth Marfa House," *Big Bend Sentinel* (Marfa, TX), January 31, 2002.

22. For a complete list of past residents, see http://www.lannan.org/resi dency/past/. Although mainly host to writers, the Lannan Foundation has also periodically hosted artists and translators.

23. Sterry Butcher, "New Group Will Renovate Building, Serve Women Artists," *Big Bend Sentinel* (Marfa, TX), July 3, 2002.

24. Sterry Butcher, "Marfa's Newest Cultural Space Offers Alternative Scene," *Big Bend Sentinel* (Marfa, TX), April 22, 2004.

25. Bill Davenport, "Ballroom Marfa Drive-In Project 'Deferred,'" *Glasstire*, June 11, 2014.

26. Source: http://www.aynfoundation.com.

27. As told to me by Tim Crowley.

28. Andy Langer, "Tiny, Remote Marfa Poised to Be a Rock-Star Magnet," *New York Times*, October 1, 2011.

29. Stirling Kelso, "Four Hotels with Spice, Allure and the Liz Lambert Touch," *New York Times*, March 26, 2011.

30. "Liz Lambert," *Texas Monthly*, February 2008.

31. Liz Lambert presented her El Cosmico project to a 2006 UT Austin real estate management course taught by Steve Ross. Other UT Austin classes have contributed to design projects.

32. The Hotel Paisano has forty-one rooms; the Thunderbird Hotel has twenty-four rooms; the Riata Inn has twenty rooms; El Cosmico has eight rooms between its eight trailers, yurts, and teepees, but a large camping ground; and the Arcón Inn has five rooms. The new Hotel Saint George has fifty-five rooms.

33. Jan Buchholz, "Austin Hotelier Liz Lambert Signs Big Investment Deal," *Austin Business Journal*, July 16, 2015.

34. A reading at the Marfa Book Company could turn out thirty people, while a lecture at the Crowley Theater could see one hundred attendees. On a slow night at Padre's, there may only be ten people listening to the live band. During big weekends, Marfa's population of two thousand often doubles.

35. http://crowleytheater.org.

36. Sue Beeton, "Landscapes as Characters: Film, Tourism, and a Sense of Place." *Metro Magazine* 166, Special Feature Section on Landscape and Location in Australian Cinema (2010), 114–119; quote from p. 114.

37. http://marfalocations.com.

38. Emily McCullar, "What Does the New Show *I Love Dick* Say about Marfa?," *Texas Monthly*, August 26, 2016.

39. Source: http://www.marfafilmfestival.com.

40. Source: http://www.cinemarfa.org/about.

41. Source: http://www.cinemarfa.org.

42. These are 2011 prices.

43. "Interview with Lineaus Lorette," interview by Jason Oslo Kolker and Rose Anderson-Lewis, *Marfa Oral History Project*, Marfa Public Radio, August 28, 2012.

44. Interview with Charles Mary Kubricht, Marfa, 2011; she was quoting a local boy.

45. Adam Weaver, "Tourism and the Military: Pleasure and the War Economy," *Annals of Tourism Research* 38, no. 2 (2011): 672–689; Valene Smith, "War and Tourism: An American Ethnography," *Annals of Tourism Research* 25, no. 1 (1998): 202–227.

46. Interview with Marianne Stockebrand, Marfa, 2011.

47. See Edward W. Said, *Orientalism* (New York: Vintage Books, 1979); Denis E. Cosgrove, *Geography and Vision: Seeing, Imagining and Representing the World* (London: I. B. Tauris, 2008); K. Maria D. Lane, *Geographies of Mars: Seeing and Knowing the Red Planet* (Chicago: University of Chicago Press, 2011).

48. From Anatole Broyard: "We are all tourists in history, and irony is what we win in wars." Dean MacCannell, *The Tourist: A New Theory of the Leisure Class* (New York: Schocken, 1976), 9.

49. Cohane, "52 Places to Go in 2016."

50. Monica Wheelock, "Art Transforming Texas Desert Town into Cultural Oasis," *University Wire*, October 9, 2007.

51. Cameron Dodd, "County Adopts Homestead Property Tax Exemption," *Big Bend Sentinel* (Marfa, TX), April 28, 2016.

52. Rachel Monroe, "More Guests, Empty Houses," *Slate*, February 13, 2014.

53. See the 2014 US Census.

54. From a letter to the editor in the *Big Bend Sentinel*, January 20, 2005.

55. Michael Barnes, "There's More to Marfa Than Mysterious Lights and Vibrant Arts Scene," *Austin-American Statesman*, March 25, 2008.

CHAPTER 6. CONCLUSION

1. Sterry Butcher, "Service Saturday for Donald Judd," *Big Bend Sentinel* (Marfa, TX), February 17, 1994.

2. Though not discussed in this book, Judd had acquired nearly 40,000 acres of ranch land in the surrounding Chihuahuan Desert. The Judd Foundation maintains these ranches, although they are not available for public tours.

3. Interview with Cecilia Thompson, Marfa, 2011.

4. Interview with Rob Weiner, Marfa, 2011.

5. There are too many grants to name here, but Chinati's website has an exhaustive list of over sixty major supporters; see www.chinati.org /information/funding.php.

6. Stockebrand, Judd, and Fuchs, *Chinati*.

7. Paul de la Garza, "A Nuclear Waste Dump Becomes a Border Issue," *Chicago Tribune*, October 19, 1998; Rick Lyman, "For Some, Texas Town Is Too Popular as Waste Disposal Site," *New York Times*, September 2, 1998; Tom Haines, "Air Force Changing Bomber Training Runs over Far West Texas," *Big Bend Sentinel* (Marfa, TX), January 20, 2011; Tom Haines, "Ranchers Challenge Air Force Plans for Bomber Routes," *Big Bend Sentinel* (Marfa, TX), January 27, 2011; Cameron Dodd, "Feds Approve Pipeline, Opposition Talks Next Moves," *Big Bend Sentinel* (Marfa, TX), May 6, 2016.

8. See Michael Hitchcock and Ken Teague, *Souvenirs: The Material Culture of Tourism* (Aldershot, Hants, UK: Ashgate, 2000); Hugh Wilkins, "Souvenirs: What and Why We Buy," *Journal of Travel Research* 50, no. 3 (2011): 239–247; and Mary Ann Littrell, Luella F. Anderson, and Pamela

J. Brown, "What Makes a Craft Souvenir Authentic?," *Annals of Tourism Research* 20, no. 1 (1993): 197–215.

9. Peter-Paul Verbeek, *What Things Do: Philosophical Reflections on Technology, Agency, and Design* (University Park: Pennsylvania State University Press, 2005).

10. I'm taking a leap here, because my request to *Marfa Journal* on the source of the name was not returned. So it could be a Russian source, but I doubt it.

11. Sources: https://www.madewell.com/madewell_category/BAGS/cross bodybags/PRDOVR~01149/01149.jsp and https://www.madewell.com /madewell_category/BAGS/crossbodybags/PRDOVR~01147/01147 .jsp. In 2017 Madewell released a second collection of "Marfa" bags and wallets.

12. http://www.midcenturymarfa.com.

13. http://shop-freda.com/pages/frontpage.

14. mirthmarfa.com.

15. Although the number of sales tax permits in Marfa in recent years is alarming: 2009: 1; 2010: 26; 2011: 14; 2012: 17; 2013: 24. Source: Texas Comptroller.

16. http://www.designmarfa.com.

17. http://www.marfadialogues.org.

18. Quoting Marfa Mayor David Lanman in Andrew Nelson and Stephanie Corley, "Showdown in Marfa," *Salon*, August 1, 2005, http://www .salon.com/2005/08/01/marfa.

19. Alberto Tomas Halpern, "Playboy to Erect Sculpture near Marfa," *Big Bend Sentinel* (Marfa, TX), May 30, 2013, accessed July 2, 2013, http:// bigbendnow.com/2013/05/move-over-prada-marfa-playboy-plans-outdoor-sculpture/.

20. Alberto Tomas Halpern, "Playboy Reveals All about Installation," *Big Bend Sentinel* (Marfa, TX), June 20, 2013.

21. Ibid.

22. Francesca Mari, "What Is Art? Can a Bunny in the Desert Tell Us?," *Texas Monthly*, November 2013.

23. See http://www.fhwa.dot.gov/real_estate/oac/oacprog.cfm#ACT1958.

24. Lawrence Wright, "Lady Bird's Lost Legacy," *New York Times*, July 20, 2007.

25. Francesca Mari, "Maybe This Is Why Warhol Stuck to Soup Cans," *New York Times*, September 14, 2013. However, Texas DOT has not ordered its removal and is not expected to. Its creators maintain that there is a difference between using a logo in a piece of art that is not paid for by the corporation and using a logo in a piece of art this is paid for by the corporation.

26. Sarah Vasquez, "With Help of Attorney DeGuerin, Playboy Bunny Remains Standing," *Big Bend Sentinel* (Marfa, TX), August 15, 2013.

27. Terry Wallace, "'Playboy Marfa' Bunny Logo to Be Moved to Dallas Museum," Associated Press, November 15, 2013.

28. Eric Aasen, "Prada Marfa Finds a Way to Stay Open: It's an Art Museum," *KERA News*, September 15, 2014.

29. John Daniel Garcia, "LGBTQ Rights: A National Struggle, a Local Acceptance," *Big Bend Sentinel* (Marfa, TX), April 28, 2016; and Chelsey Trahan, "Marfa ISD Adding Gender Neutral Restroom for Transgender Student," *NewsWest9.com*, May 17, 2016.

30. Emily Jo Cureton, "Occupy Movement Comes to Marfa, Alpine," *Big Bend Sentinel* (Marfa, TX), October 27, 2011.

31. John Daniel Garcia, "Locals to Join Post-inauguration Marches in D.C., Austin," *Big Bend Sentinel* (Marfa, TX), January 19, 2017.

32. Sean Wilsey, "Marfa, Revisited," in *More Curious* (San Francisco: McSweeney's, 2014), 323.

INDEX